THE TROUT COOK

THE TROUT COOK

100 Ways with Trout

PATRICIA ANN HAYES

The Crowood Press

First published in 1989 by
The Crowood Press
Ramsbury, Marlborough
Wiltshire SN8 2HE

British Library Cataloguing in Publication Data

Hayes, Patricia Ann
    The trout cook
    1. Food. Trout dishes. Recipes
    I. Title
    641.6'92

    ISBN 1 85223 130 0

Dedication

With love to my husband, with whom I share the fascination of fishing, and
without whom I would have no useable fishing tackle.

Acknowledgements

Line diagrams by Claire Upsdale-Jones
Line drawings by Rodger McPhail

Typeset by Qualitext Typesetting, Abingdon
Printed in Great Britain by Billing & Sons Ltd, Worcester

Contents

PREFACE

I walked around a peaceful trout lake one autumn afternoon, obliged to put away rod and reel for a week, having reached my limit. I considered whether I could devise some original way of serving trout for the second time this week, or would my catch just be added to an already bulging deep-freeze? The season had been a good one. I wondered what other anglers did with all their fish – I knew that many of them moved on to other waters once they had had their limit here.

I paused to chat to one or two on the way and introduced two questions discreetly into the conversation: 'Have you a favourite way of cooking trout? What do you do with so many fish?' They nearly always came out with the same sort of answer: 'Get a bit bored with them; give most of 'em away. Even eating them once a week can be a bit much.' I had to admit that even my family and friends were getting bored with them too!

On a subsequent occasion I was watching one of the syndicate members playing an obviously strong fish, with rod well and truly bent. He landed a splendid 4½lb trout which was duly admired. After weighing it and putting it in the records, he said to me, 'Would you like it? There's only the wife and I and it's too big for us.' I hesitated, not knowing whether to accept or reject his kind offer and then asked, 'Would you let me cold smoke it? That way we could have half each.' I was delighted when he agreed, and in due course he was amazed at the transformation of his fish into 'smoked salmon'.

The seed of an idea was growing – how to get more pleasure from these lovely fish after the enjoyment of catching them, and how to share them in ways that could continually surprise and delight all those who had said, 'Not trout again!'

I hope that the material researched and the recipes here (both devised and collected) will add extra to the appreciation of the trout of yourself, your angling partner and your friends.

Patricia Hayes

INTRODUCTION

Until the advent of commercial fish farming, the occasional fresh trout was regarded as a rare delicacy. Even the most simple methods of cooking – frying, grilling or poaching – were, and still are, more than adequate to achieve the basis of a delightful meal, which would be easily digested and have as much protein value as its equivalent in fillet steak.

Over-fishing and pollution of the sea have depleted natural stocks of fish alarmingly; there are too many nations hunting too few fish in disputed territories. It is likely that in the future much of our demand for fish will be met by commercial fish farms.

Trout are reared nowadays not only for food but for the extensive sporting market as well. More and more ponds, lakes and reservoirs in all parts of the country are being stocked to meet the requirements of the trout angler. It is not unusual for his boundless enthusiasm for this hobby to 'net' him anything from one to five hundred fish in a season. Some may be sold to help with the cost of tickets, licences and equipment, some will perhaps be bartered in exchange for meat or game, but most will be given away after the inevitable boredom that comes with eating too much of a good thing. The angler's palate can no longer be tempted by them.

As I am both a game fisherman and a cook, it was this aspect which stimulated my curiosity for presenting the trout in as many varied ways as possible and made me realise the need for such a book. Some one hundred recipes, devised, adapted and collected, are brought together here under one cover for your enjoyment.

In order to produce a wide variety of dishes it is necessary to learn three basic skills: filleting, hot smoking and cold smoking. Each of these is dealt with before the recipes themselves. There follows a section covering a wide range of suitable sauces, and lastly, the problem of what vegetables to serve with fish is tackled in a comprehensive list, along with suggested methods of preparation.

CLEANING AND FILLETING

Gutting

Many of the following recipes call for the fish to be left whole, with or without head and tail, and only require it to be gutted. To do this, simply

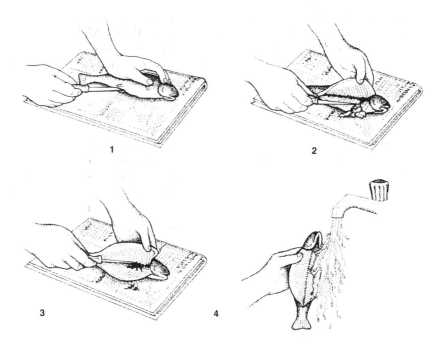

Fig 1 Gutting and cleaning.

cut with a sharp pointed knife from the vent along the belly and well into the gills. Pull out the innards, paying careful attention to the blood along the backbone which can be easily scraped away with a dessertspoon. Wash the fish under a cold running tap. If the skin is to be eaten (and, in certain methods of cooking, it is very tasty), it should be scrubbed to remove slime. Whilst washing the fish under running water, draw the blade of a kitchen knife against the lie of the scales until the skin looks and feels scale-free.

Filleting Uncooked Trout

A fish weighing over a pound, which you may wish to share between two persons, is so much easier to eat filleted. Once you have mastered filleting you may more often than not choose to prepare your fish in this way, and it will be essential if you want to smoke larger fish. First, cut off the head and tail, gut the fish as described and lay it, slit open towards you, on newspaper to prevent it slipping. Start at the shoulder and place the point of a sharp kitchen knife between the bones and flesh of the bottom fillet. Cut with clean strokes as close to the bones as possible, until the whole fillet lies flat away from the backbone. Turn the fish over and repeat for the second fillet. From the tail end the backbone can be gently eased and lifted away leaving the two fillets still joined by the skin. They may now be reassembled as a whole fish, opened out and coated for frying, or detached into separate fillets. It may take several attempts and a little wasted flesh to perfect the skill, but it *is* simple once mastered.

When you are frying fillets it is essential to fry the skin side first, otherwise the fish will curl awkwardly in the pan. Once the skin side has had two or three minutes' cooking, turn the fish over, flesh side down, until it is cooked through. If required, the skin may be easily peeled off with the aid of a knife whilst the flesh side is cooking. The flesh of the trout is not as firm as that of many white fish and care must be taken in lifting a fillet without its skin, to keep it intact.

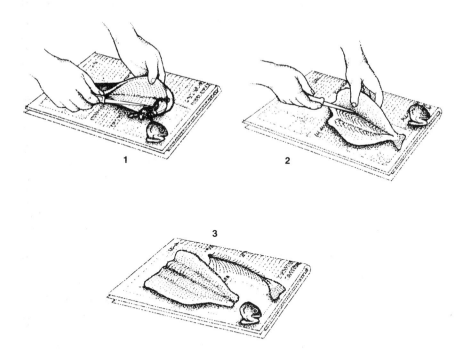

Fig 2 Boning and filleting.

Filleting Cooked Trout

Where cooked whole trout are to be served cold, having been either hot smoked or poached, it is usual to retain the head and tail for presentation purposes. To fillet, carefully remove the skin, then slit down along the backbone, loosening it on both sides. Nick through the backbone at head and tail end with scissors. Gently pull out the bone, starting at the tail end, and ease away the flesh taking care not to damage it.

Boning

Slit the belly from the vent well into the gills and remove guts. Open cavity as wide as possible. With the points of a pair of kitchen scissors snip through backbone at head and tail. Loosen the rib cage bones from the flesh with the point of a sharp knife. Ease away and lift out the skeleton. The boneless fish is now ready for reassembling as a whole and stuffing as required by the recipe of your choice.

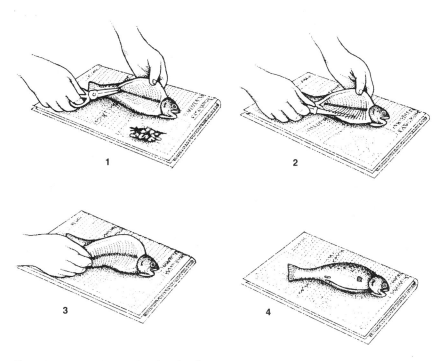

Fig 3 Boning out, leaving head and tail intact.

STORAGE

Fresh trout should be gutted and washed within a few hours of being caught and may be kept in the refrigerator for up to two days before being cooked.

Fish not required for fairly immediate use should be deep frozen. They should be gutted and cleaned, leaving the head and tail intact, placed in polythene bags, and sealed with as much air excluded as possible to prevent the flesh drying out. If, for any reason, it is inconvenient to remove the innards, the fish may be stored with these intact. When partially thawed out it will be possible to slit the belly and pull out the innards in a fairly tidy lump. Be careful to scrape the blood away from the backbone when the fish is fully thawed. If you are gutting a large batch of fish at a time the innards may be wrapped in newspaper and placed in the freezer until the day of refuse collection.

Frozen trout should remain in peak condition for 3–6 months, after which time they may lose some of their flavour and are best smoked. Do not keep any fish for longer than 9 months. It is a good idea to mark bags with the date that the fish were caught, so that those frozen early in the season may be used up first.

Fish required for hot or cold smoking must first be thawed thoroughly, and after smoking they may be frozen again for approximately 6 months. Before being frozen they should be wrapped in clear film, then thoroughly sealed in a double layer of foil, otherwise their smokiness may permeate other foods in the freezer.

Before having a hot smoking session it is worth while waiting until you have collected a number of fish in the freezer. This way you will be able to select a quantity of suitable size for hot smoking a good batch at a time. You may then deep freeze those not required immediately, and use them later, either cold in salads or reheated in the various ways described in the following recipes. Similarly, it is best to wait until you have collected in the freezer a number of larger-sized fish before embarking on a cold smoking session. The cold-smoked fish should be divided into individual fillets and trimmed of any surplus fat, skin and fins before being individually wrapped in clear film and double foil — whether being frozen or refrigerated — to prevent other foods being tainted.

To achieve versatility and variety you can treat your trout in six different ways:

- Cook from fresh
- Freeze from fresh
- Freeze poached
- Freeze hot-smoked
- Freeze cold-smoked
- Freeze certain ready-made dishes

You will also achieve savings in time and money.

HOT SMOKING

The action of cooking with smoke and heat imparts to the trout a very fine distinctive flavour and greatly adds to the variety of dishes the cook can produce. I hope the reader will be persuaded that it is not complex, and that it is an incredibly worthwhile process which turns the ordinary into the exceptional. It is very inexpensive to use a home smoker and it represents a completely fat-free method of cooking.

The basic equipment you will need is a metal box to act as a smoke oven. This will be raised (for example, on legs or bricks), to enable a source of concentrated heat to be put under it. The sources of heat can be methylated spirits, solid cooking blocks, a picnic gas burner, charcoal, or even a gas cooker indoors; however, outdoor cooking is recommended, preferably on a dry day with no more than a light breeze. If you are doing indoor cooking, you will need a good extractor fan, otherwise you may end up with a rather pungent house for a day or two! As well as your smoke oven, you will require some hardwood sawdust. This can often be purchased at a very modest cost from a timber merchant and it is also stocked by most fishing tackle shops. Oak or beech sawdust is best, but it is also worth considering sawdust from old fruitwoods which imparts its own particular flavour. One word of warning — never use softwoods, as these cause an unpleasant and resinous taste.

Smoke ovens and boxes of various designs are manufactured and sold through angling shops and mail-order catalogues, but it is a wise idea to experiment with hot smoking before making your purchase of a sturdy commercial home smoker. In this way, you will also find out which size is most suitable for your requirements.

Basically, if you can find a wire grid to fit a rectangular biscuit tin, and some hardwood sawdust, then, using foil as your 'baffle' plate, you have all the equipment needed.

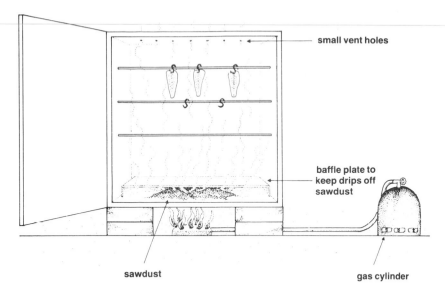

small vent holes

baffle plate to
keep drips off
sawdust

sawdust

gas cylinder

Fig 4 Hot smoker cabinet, run on gas.

Method

First clean and gut the required number of fish, leaving their heads
on. Season the inside of the fish only as salt on the skin will cause it to
peel. Dry the fish with absorbent kitchen paper and place them on the
rack. Scatter wood sawdust evenly over the base of your smoker box – in
a small box you will require between one and three heaped tablespoons-
ful, depending on the strength of smoke flavour preferred. Protect the
sawdust from drips by a loose baffle plate (make one from aluminium foil
if you don't have one), and place the rack into the box. There should be a
good amount of air space all around the fish so that the smoke can
circulate freely. Put the lid on the box. Light the source of heat (for
example, methylated spirits or a solid fuel tablet), and allow to burn for 3
or 4 minutes, then place the supported box about 6.5cm/2½in above
the heat. Leave to cook for approximately 20 minutes for a small
275–400g/10–14oz fish. Test with the point of a knife to make sure that
the fish is cooked properly – if the flesh is ready to part from the bones,
it is done. The fish may then be served hot or cold.

CURING

The art of curing by first salting and then smoking is the oldest known method of preserving meat and fish. The key to good flavour lies in curing the fish, either in brine solution or by the dry curing method, prior to smoking. This will harden the skin so that it will not tear when hung, and firms the flesh to facilitate fine slicing. The salt and spices in the brine will combine with the smoke to create the unique flavour we associate with smoked foods. Although long-term salting tends to harden food and is essential for long-term preservation without refrigeration, the short periods of brining or dry curing suggested here will in fact tenderise the flesh. Having removed the heads (fairly high up), fillet the fish carefully so that they are ready for curing. Do not separate the pairs of fillets at this stage.

Equipment

Any stout tub or wide-bottomed basin can be used as a brine bath, but if you want to do a good deal of brining and smoking it is worth obtaining or finding a special container for the process. An old-style glazed ceramic sink with a waste outlet in the bottom is ideal. When you have finished brining, you can let the brine run out into a suitable storage vessel. As a rule, a basic brine can be used several times before it becomes scummy and unfit for use.

Brine Cure

4.5 litres/1 gallon water
2 tablespoons onion salt
2 tablespoons garlic salt
juice of one lemon
225g/8oz dark brown sugar
450g/1lb cooking salt

Mix thoroughly in a deep vessel, making sure all salts and sugar are dissolved; use cold. Soak for 1–4 hours, according to taste and the size of your fillets; pat with absorbent kitchen paper and hang up in an area free from dust and flies until completely dry. It will not matter if the fillets are left hanging overnight, ready for smoking next morning, as long as they are in a cool place. Lightly paint all surfaces of the fish with olive oil or light vegetable oil before smoking to prevent further drying.

Dry Cure

Instead of brining, excellent results can be obtained by laying the fillets, still in pairs, on large dishes or trays and covering them with a mixture of 2 parts common salt to 1 part soft brown sugar. You will need about 4 tablespoons of the mixture for each 1.5kg/3lb of fish. Sprinkle a thick layer on the tray, lay the fish skin side down and sprinkle the remainder on top. The mixture will soon become a syrupy liquid. Leave for 3–4 hours, depending on the size of fish, basting the fish with the liquid two or three times during the process. Wash the fillets thoroughly under cold running water and hang up to dry on hooks as illustrated until completely dry in a cool, dust- and insect-free place, overnight if desired. Finally, lightly coat fillets with olive oil.

COLD SMOKING

Cold smoking really means 'almost cold' smoking. Food is not cooked in the heat and smoke from a nearby fire as it is in hot smoking. It is first cured, then gently wrapped in cool smoke from a fire nearby, so that the resins and other elements of the smoke penetrate into every part of the food without altering its structure. In other words, its fat does not melt.

It is really not worth cold smoking a trout under 900g/2lb as the fillets from this size of fish will be too thin. However, anything over this weight, preferably with a good pink flesh, is as good, if not better, than some commercially-produced smoked salmon, and can be served with great confidence (and even some dishonesty!).

Equipment

A receptacle is needed to allow the fish to hang in an area of concentrated smoke for some 3–4 hours; the fish must be sufficiently far away from the source of heat not to cook.

Note   The temperature around the fish must not rise above 32°C/90°F.

There are a number of cold smokers commercially available and although somewhat expensive they are a wise investment as the running costs are negligible. However, it is also quite feasible to make your own cold smoker, with a little ingenuity. Some basic ideas are sketched here, ranging from a converted galvanised dustbin with a rubber lid to cabinets with direct or indirect heat and the chimney flue type which I use. Certain imported cold smokers are available through larger fishing tackle shops. These are comparatively expensive.

We constructed a portable smoker (*see* Fig 6) which can be kept in a shed or garage when not in use. The chimney was a length of second-hand flue lining purchased from a local scrap dealer, and an old metal deed box from the same source became the fire box. This was welded to the flue near the base having a hole cut through to the 'chimney'. All the edges and joints were well sealed to exclude as much draught as possible. When we were using the oven it was placed on several sheets of newspaper to catch the drips below the chimney (which was deliberately left open-ended to avoid any cleaning problems), but it could also have been bedded in sand or soil. A damp cloth over the top of the chimney retained a sufficient volume of concentrated smoke.

As a permanent fixture in the garden, a smoke oven can be constructed in brick in an exaggerated 'L' shape. Part of the horizontal section, for the fire, will need a heavy metal lid to exclude draught and to prevent the fire becoming too hot. The vertical section will need to be approximately 4ft (120cm) high and open-ended, with rods across from which to suspend the fish from hooks (*see* Fig 6 for these, which can be simply constructed from pieces of wire coathanger). Again, a damp cloth over the stack retains the smoke.

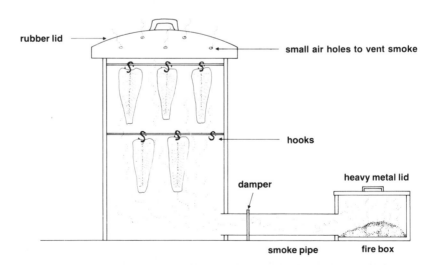

Fig 5 Cold smoker made at home from a dustbin.

18

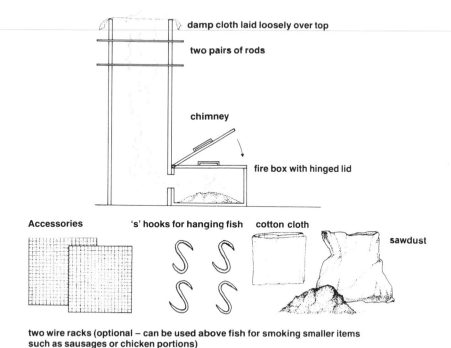

damp cloth laid loosely over top

two pairs of rods

chimney

fire box with hinged lid

Accessories   's' hooks for hanging fish   cotton cloth

sawdust

two wire racks (optional – can be used above fish for smoking smaller items such as sausages or chicken portions)

Fig 6 Home-made portable cold smoker made from second-hand flue lining and an old metal deed box, both acquired from a local scrap dealer.

Whatever equipment you use, the source of smoke comes from smouldering hardwood sawdust. Oak, beech or other hardwoods can be used, but never use softwoods which impart a tarry, resinous flavour. Don't use softwoods to light the fire initially, or firelighters; paper and small sticks chipped from hardwood logs are best. The principle is the same – to envelop your cured fish in cool smoke for a few hours.

Method

Light a fire in the firebox, either with hardwood sticks or charcoal, and tend this until it has achieved a good hot base from which the flames have subsided. Dampen this down with sawdust and wait until a good volume of smoke is produced. Close down the lid tightly – draughts will cause the sawdust to burn too fiercely instead of smouldering.

Having previously oiled the fish and placed a secure hook at the top of each, suspend them from the rods at the top of the chimney (or on racks, following the maker's instructions if a box is used). Check the fire and

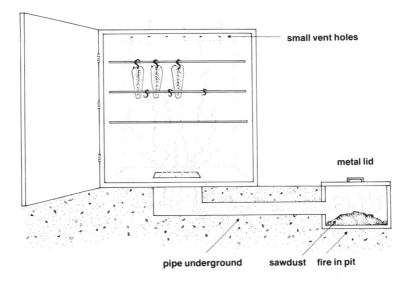

small vent holes

metal lid

pipe underground   sawdust   fire in pit

Fig 7 Cold smoker cabinet.

top up with sawdust if necessary – a good volume of smoke should be issuing from the chimney. Cover this with a damp cloth. It will be necessary to tend the fire and top up with sawdust every 45 minutes.

Length of smoking time is a matter of taste but it should not be less than 2 hours for small fish and needs to be around 3–4 hours for larger ones. Under-smoking produces a disappointing flavour, while you will be unlikely to hear complaints about an over-smoked taste.

Finally, remove the fish and divide the pairs into individual fillets. Trim these of any surplus fat and skin and then wrap them in clear film. It is recommended that any fish cured and smoked by the methods described should be double wrapped and stored in the deep-freeze if not required for eating within four or five days. The fillets thaw out ready for use in an hour or so from removal from the freezer, and it is also possible to cut very fine slices just before the flesh has fully thawed.

If you haven't mutilated the fish when filleting initially, there will remain one row of bones about two-thirds of the way down the thickest part of each fillet – the 'pin' bones. They could be removed by cutting out a 'V' channel of fish and bones, but raw trout is too delicate for this. With the slight shrinkage which occurs during smoking some of them may be seen to protrude. They are easy to feel, and can simply be pulled out, with fingers or tweezers, in the direction from tail to head. This will facilitate carving.

CHAPTER 1

ENTRÉES

Trout-Stuffed Green Peppers

Serves 8 (or 4 as a main course)   Preparation time: 15 minutes   Cooking time: 45 minutes

(Preparation time presumes that you have some ready-poached trout to hand. As mentioned in the introduction, if you have a surplus of fish at any time you can treat them in a variety of ways prior to freezing.)

4 medium green peppers
1 medium onion, chopped
25g/1oz butter
1 cup grated fresh breadcrumbs
225g/8oz cooked trout flesh
Worcester sauce
salt and ground black pepper

Pre-heat the oven to 200°C/400°F/Gas Mark 6.

1 Blanch green peppers in salted water for about 7 minutes until becoming tender. Gently remove from pan. Plunge into cold water to refresh.

2 Fry the onion in a little butter, toss in the breadcrumbs, trout flesh and seasoning, and mix well.

3 Carefully cut the peppers in half lengthwise, remove seeds and pack with the breadcrumb mixture. Dot with butter and place in an earthenware casserole.

4 Bake in moderate oven, uncovered, for 25–30 minutes.

Serving suggestion: Serve one half on a slice of crisp fried bread as a starter, or as a main course serve two each, topped with piped mashed potato and accompanied by baked whole tomatoes.

Smoked Trout Soufflé

Serves 6 (or 4 as a main course)   Preparation time: 20 minutes   Cooking time: 40 minutes

This dish is suitable not only as an entrée, but also as a main course, with the appropriate vegetables.

50g/2oz butter
1 tablespoon grated parmesan
50g/2oz plain flour
275ml/½ pint boiling milk,
    seasoned with bay leaf, cloves
    and mace
cayenne pepper

salt
150g/6oz finely flaked hot-
    smoked trout
4 egg yolks
5 egg whites
40g/1½oz grated Cheddar cheese

Pre-heat the oven to 200°C/400°F/Gas Mark 6.

1   Butter a 1.4 litre/2½ pint soufflé dish and sprinkle parmesan around the edges and base.

2   Melt remaining butter in a pan, add the flour, cook for 2 minutes, lower heat and slowly stir in the boiling milk (straining off seasoning ingredients). Season with cayenne and salt. When sauce is thickened continue to boil for two minutes, stirring continuously. Add flaked fish and remove from the heat.

3   Beat egg yolks into mixture one by one. Allow to cool a little.

4   Beat egg whites until stiff. Mix a little egg white into the sauce, add the Cheddar then carefully fold in the rest of the whites taking care not to knock the air out. Pour into soufflé dish.

5   Place soufflé in the centre of the pre-heated oven and cook for 5 minutes. Turn the heat down slightly and continue to cook for about 30 minutes. The soufflé should be well risen and brown on top. Serve immediately – as it cools it will flop.

Serving suggestion: Serve with crispy sauté potatoes and a green side salad, or on its own as an entrée.

Savoury Stuffed Eggs

Serves 6   Preparation time: 10 minutes   Cooking time: 10 minutes

Eggs stuffed with hot-smoked or cold-smoked trout make a simple entrée, or small eggs can be used as canapés.

6 medium eggs
175g/6oz hot- or cold-smoked
   trout, or smoked salmon pieces
2 tablespoons salad cream
tabasco
paprika
salt

1 Hard-boil eggs for 10 minutes and plunge immediately into cold water to prevent discoloration of yolks.

2 Flake the flesh from the trout.

3 Shell and halve the eggs when cool and remove yolks. Place the yolks, trout, salad cream and seasonings in a blender for a few seconds, or mash together well with a fork. Pile back into egg halves, or pipe back decoratively.

Serving suggestion: Serve as an entrée on crisp lettuce with fine tomato and cucumber slices.

Stuffed Tomatoes

Serves 8   Preparation time: 20 minutes   Cooking time: 25 minutes

These can be prepared well in advance and could be cooked on the shelf below the roast to make life easier for the hostess.

8 medium, firm tomatoes
1 large onion, sliced
1 cup cooked rice
1 tablespoon tomato purée
1 cup smoked trout flesh, flaked
milled black pepper and salt
25g/1oz butter

Pre-heat the oven to 190°C/375°F/Gas Mark 5 (or cook below joint in hotter oven).

1 Cut tops off tomatoes and scoop out flesh.

2 Fry onion in a little butter until golden. Combine tomato flesh with other ingredients, season and pack into tomato shells.

3 Dot with butter and bake for about 25 minutes, or until soft and browned on top.

Serving suggestion: Cut white bread circles with a pastry cutter, fry until golden in butter and place a baked tomato on each circle.

Smoked Trout Pâté

Serves 8   Preparation time: 15 minutes

An entrée dish using your own hot-smoked trout; this can also be purchased from trout farms or freezer shops. A little pot of smoked trout pâté makes a very acceptable gift.

450g/1lb hot-smoked trout
225g/8oz cream cheese or low fat
    curd cheese
juice of 1 lemon
ground sea salt
ground black pepper

---

1 Remove the skin and bones from the trout and place the flesh, cream cheese, lemon juice and seasoning in a blender. Process until smooth.

---

2 Pack into individual oiled ramekin dishes. Refrigerate for at least an hour before serving.

Note   Should you wish to freeze this dish, substitute half the cream cheese with melted butter, otherwise when thawed the pâté will tend to crumble instead of remaining smooth.

Baked Trout Terrine

Serves 8   Preparation time: 30 minutes   Cooking time: 1 hour

A dish which can be made in advance and kept refrigerated for a few days, but which does not freeze well.

700g/2lb trout flesh	*1 teaspoon tabasco*
2 egg yolks	*nutmeg*
100g/4oz butter (melted)	*cayenne*
75g/3oz flour	*salt*
150ml/¼ pint milk	*200ml/7oz thick cream*
50g/2oz mushrooms, chopped	*40ml/1½fl oz white vermouth*
1 shallot, chopped	*50g/2oz butter*

Pre-heat the oven to 190°C/375°F/Gas Mark 5.

1   Put egg yolks in a saucepan, pour on half the melted butter and beat vigorously. Sprinkle on flour and continue to beat until completely incorporated. Add milk very gradually to avoid lumps, and continue to beat.

2   Place over gentle heat, stirring until thickened. Add seasonings and mix well.

3   Melt 25g/1oz butter in another saucepan; sauté the mushrooms, shallots and herbs over a low heat until soft.

4   Purée the fish in a blender, add remainder of melted butter, the seasoned sauce, vegetables, cream and vermouth.

5   Butter the base and sides of a terrine dish or loaf tin and pour mixture into dish. Cover with two thicknesses of aluminium kitchen foil. Place the dish in a bain-marie (larger tin), filled half-way with boiling water.

6   Place in oven and bake for an hour. Insert a skewer – if it comes out clean, the terrine is cooked. Allow to cool, then refrigerate for at least 8 hours before serving.

Serving suggestion: Serve in very thin slices with a shrimp sauce (*see* page 120) and brown bread and butter.

Two Trout Canapés

Plain and smoked trout mini-rolls of which two, garnished suitably, would make an individual entrée. Preparation time depends on your store of poached and cold-smoked trout. To cut time but increase cost, you could buy ready-sliced smoked salmon.

*1 wafer-thin slice of smoked
    salmon or cold-smoked trout
    per portion*
*1 tablespoonful flaked poached
    trout per portion*
*1 dessertspoonful thick natural
    yoghurt per portion*
*lemon juice, sea salt and paprika
    to season yoghurt*

1 Mix the poached trout, yoghurt and seasonings and bind together.

2 Take a thin slice of smoked fish. Lay a line of filling down the centre and roll up. If the rolls are too long to be picked up daintily, cut each in half, into bite-size pieces.

To serve as an entrée: Allow approximately 50g/2oz per person and serve with finely sliced cucumber, vinaigrette and brown bread and butter.

Trout with Mushrooms in Puff Pastry Cases

Serves 8   Preparation time: 20 minutes   Cooking time: 30 minutes

Use of convenience foods makes this quick and simple to produce. The dish can also be served in larger quantities as a main course.

225g/8oz ready-poached trout flesh
1 tin condensed mushroom soup
1 tin tiny button mushrooms

1 teaspoon dried mixed herbs
salt and black pepper
225g/8oz pack puff pastry
1 egg yolk for glaze

Pre-heat the oven to 230°F/450°C/Gas Mark 8.

---

1 Flake the fish finely, removing all skin and bones. Combine with the mushroom soup, mushrooms, dried mixed herbs and seasoning to taste.

---

2 Cut block of pastry into four with a very sharp knife. Roll each quarter out as large and thin as practical, and then cut each into two, making eight squares.

---

3 Put a portion of filling into the centre of each square. Fold up the sides and crimp edges to encase filling. Place on a greased oven tray, brush tops with egg yolk and bake in the hot oven for 10 minutes. Reduce heat and continue to bake for a further 15–20 minutes until golden-brown.

Serving suggestion: Serve one per person as an entrée, garnished with a sprig of watercress, or two per person as a main course, with buttery creamed potato and french beans.

Potted Trout and Prawns

Serves 4–6   Preparation time: 25 minutes   Cooking time: 10 minutes

This makes an ideal entrée and you can easily multiply the quantities for a buffet table dish.

2 small trout, washed and gutted
bunch of parsley
2 thick slices lemon (keep
*   remainder for juice)*
100g/4oz shelled prawns
2 teaspoons horseradish sauce
salt and pepper
150g/5oz clarified butter

1   Put parsley into a wide pan and lay the trout on top. Add a couple of thick slices of lemon, cut from the centre (reserve end pieces for juice). Pour on boiling water to cover and simmer for 10 minutes.

2   Drain and cool. Discard the parsley and lemon then skin and bone the fish, breaking it up into flakes. Chop the prawns roughly and mix with the flaked trout, horseradish sauce, lemon juice, salt, pepper and half the clarified butter.

3   Pack into four ramekin dishes and smooth down tops. Pour remaining clarified butter over to set and seal completely. Chill for at least 4 hours and serve with melba toast.

Clarified butter Use ordinary butter and melt in a small saucepan over a low heat. When it has melted, turn up heat for a minute till butter bubbles, and then remove immediately from heat. The butter will now be in three layers, with sediment on the bottom, scum on the surface, and clear in the middle. Remove scum with a spoon. Spoon the clear fat over the pâté, and discard the residue or sediment.

Melba toast (an easy method)   Buy a thick sliced loaf of bread, lightly toast on both sides of slices. Split the toast slices horizontally with a breadknife. Bake in a very slow oven for approximately ½ hour until browned through and crisp.

Smoked Trout in Avocado

Serves 4   Preparation time: 20 minutes (excluding smoking time)

This is a rather rich entrée but very delicious with either hot- or cold-smoked trout.

175g/6oz hot- or cold-smoked
  trout flesh
1 small carton sour cream
juice of half a lemon
1 drop tabasco
freshly ground black pepper
2 avocado pears
cucumber rings for garnish

1 Flake the trout flesh, removing any small bones.

2 Mix the sour cream, lemon juice, tabasco and pepper together, and add the trout flakes.

3 Cut the avocados into halves lengthwise and remove stones. Pack the trout mixture into each cavity. Slice cucumber rings almost in half, twist and decorate each portion with cucumber.

Serving suggestion: Serve with a little crisp lettuce, finely sliced red pepper rings, and buttered granary bread triangles.

Potted Smoked Trout

Serves 6   Preparation time: 25 minutes

This entrée recipe requires you to dip into your freezer store of cold-smoked trout, otherwise you will need to purchase some smoked salmon off-cuts.

200g/7oz cold-smoked trout flesh
2 hard-boiled eggs
50g/2oz Philadelphia cheese
50g/2oz melted butter
2–3 gherkins or small cucumber,
*   diced*
3 stuffed olives, sliced
paprika
juice of half a lemon
sliced tomatoes for garnish

1 Oil 6 ramekin dishes. Flake the trout flesh finely or dice with a sharp knife.

2 Separate egg yolks from whites and chop the whites finely. Combine the cheese and melted butter. Mix in the gherkins, sliced olives, paprika and lemon juice.

3 Pack into individual ramekin dishes and refrigerate for at least an hour before serving.

Serving suggestion: Turn out on to crisp shredded lettuce and decorate with chopped egg yolks and sliced tomatoes.

Smoked Trout Crêpes

Serves 6–8   Preparation time: 45 minutes   Cooking time: 25 minutes

The recipe makes 12–15 small pancakes and preparation time presumes that you have a supply of hot-smoked trout in your freezer; otherwise, add time for smoking from fresh, or purchase hot-smoked trout.

For the batter:
100g/4oz plain flour
pinch of salt
1 tablespoon vegetable oil
1 egg
1 egg yolk
275ml/½ pint milk

For the filling:
100g/¼lb sliced button
*   mushrooms*
225–350g/½–¾lb flaked smoked
*   trout*
butter or oil for frying
thick savoury sauce, made with
*   milk, fish bones, butter and*
*   flour (see page 119), or tinned*
*   ready-made sauce*
3 tablespoons double cream
50g/2oz grated parmesan cheese

Pre-heat the oven to 190°C/375°F/Gas Mark 5.

1   Sift the flour and salt into a bowl, add oil, eggs and most of the milk, beating all the time with a wooden spoon. Allow to stand for 30 minutes.

2   Fry mushrooms in butter, add to sauce, mix in flaked fish.

3   In an omelette pan fry small thin pancakes. Fill each with sauce, roll up and arrange in an open buttered dish. Pour over the cream and dust with parmesan cheese. Bake for 15 minutes.

Serving suggestion: Serve with chopped spinach and small whole baked tomatoes as a luncheon dish, or on their own as an entrée.

Green Pea and Smoked Trout Chowder

Serves 4   Preparation time: 25 minutes   Cooking time: 30 minutes

A nourishing and filling winter soup.

850ml/1½ pints water
1 fish stock cube
large tin garden peas
450g/1lb potato, diced
1 medium onion, diced
½ teaspoon sugar
lemon pepper seasoning
450g/1lb smoked trout flesh
25g/1oz cornflour
1 tablespoon double cream

1   Bring the water to the boil in a large pan. Add the stock cube and mix well. Add the peas, potato, onion, sugar and lemon pepper. Simmer for 20 minutes.

2   Chop the trout flesh into cubes.

3   Strain the stock through a sieve reserving the liquid. Thicken this liquor with the cornflour and add the strained purée.

4   Add the chopped fish to the chowder. Bring to boiling point and serve.

Serving suggestion: Swirl a little cream into each portion and serve with crusty bread.

Trout Mops

Serves 6   Preparation time: 25 minutes   Cooking time: 30 minutes

The trout version of roll mop herrings – the flavour is excellent and the flesh firmer than usual. This is a good recipe for fish suspected of being in less than perfect condition, which the angler occasionally finds at the beginning and end of the season.

6 smallish trout
1 large salad onion, finely sliced
1 tablespoon salt
1 tablespoon white pepper
425ml/¾ pint water and vinegar,
  in equal proportions
1 tablespoon brown sugar
1 tablespoon pickling spice

Pre-heat the oven to 190°C/375°F/Gas Mark 5.

---

1 Gut and fillet trout out in pairs, leaving them joined by the skin (*see* page 10 for filleting). Place a layer of raw onion on the flesh side of each fillet. Season with salt and pepper.

---

2 Roll up and secure with two cocktail sticks. Place in a deep casserole dish and cover with the liquid, sugar and pickling spice.

---

3 Bake for half an hour in the pre-heated oven and then leave to cool in the liquid. Break pairs into half, remove cocktail sticks.

Serving suggestion: Refrigerate and serve cold with a salad or as part of an hors-d'oeuvre.

Baked Avocado with Trout

Serves 4   Preparation time: 15 minutes   Cooking time: 20 minutes

An unusual hot entrée dish, particularly useful when the avocados are not ripe enough to be eaten raw.

225g/8oz poached trout flesh
1 medium onion
25g/1oz butter
2 avocado pears
juice of 1 lemon
dash of Worcester sauce
ground black pepper
sea salt
2 tablespoons fresh breadcrumbs

Pre-heat the oven to 220°C/425°F/Gas Mark 7.

---

1 Remove any skin and bones from fish and flake. Slice onion and fry in butter until opaque.

---

2 Cut avocados in half lengthwise, discard stones and scoop out flesh. Mix with lemon juice, onion, Worcester sauce, seasoning, and fish. Pile mixture back into avocado skins and press down well.

---

3 Place avocados in an earthenware dish. Sprinkle with breadcrumbs and dot with butter. Bake in the hot oven for 20 minutes.

Serving suggestion: Serve each on an individual entrée plate with Melba toast (*see* page 29).

Trout in a Leafy Parcel

Serves 4–6   Preparation time: 20 minutes   Cooking time: 10 minutes

With small trout this could make a useful entrée dish, while with larger fish it is a quick and easy main course.

4–6 trout
few sprigs of parsley
50g/2oz fresh breadcrumbs
grated rind of 1 lemon
75g/3oz melted butter
1 white cabbage leaf per fish
oil or bacon fat for frying
salt and black pepper

1 Clean, gut and de-head the trout. Chop parsley, and combine with the breadcrumbs, lemon rind and melted butter. Season with salt and pepper and fill the cavities with this mixture.

2 Blanch cabbage leaves until soft. Wrap each stuffed trout in a cabbage leaf like a parcel and secure with a cocktail stick.

3 In a heavy frying pan, fry the parcels for about 5 minutes each side, until they are well browned.

Serving suggestion: Remove sticks and serve piping hot with baked jacket potatoes and a mixed side salad.

Eggs O'Patrick

Preparation time: 5 minutes (this assumes you are able to dip into your store of ready-frozen cold-smoked trout. If not, smoked salmon pieces can be purchased.)

A very easy starter with a gourmet quality. If you are cooking a roast these can be done on the top shelf of the oven at the same time, and will only take 7–8 minutes.

1 tablespoon cold-smoked trout
*   per person, flaked*
2 dessertspoons double cream per
*   person*
1 medium egg per person
salt
paprika
chives or parsley, chopped

Pre-heat the oven to 220°C/425°F/Gas Mark 7.

1 Have to hand ramekins as required. Place cold trout pieces in ramekins, and cover with a dessertspoon of double cream.

2 Break a whole egg into the ramekin, and then season with salt. Pour remaining cream over egg and season with paprika.

3 Place ramekins on baking dish and place on high shelf in pre-heated oven. They will be ready in 7–8 minutes – the whites will just have set and the yolks will still be soft.

Serving suggestion: Garnish with parsley or chives and serve with crusty new bread.

Pressed Dilled Trout

A Scandinavian recipe for sugar-cured trout or salmon, also known as 'gravadlax'. The preparation time for this is three days, and there is no cooking involved.

900–1150g/2–3lb pink-fleshed
trout
1 large bunch of dill (or 2
tablespoons dried dill)
100g/4oz coarse salt
50g/2oz brown sugar
2 tablespoons white peppercorns,
crushed

1 Clean and bone the fish, leaving fillets joined (*see* page 10). Dry fillets with kitchen paper.

2 Mix all the other ingredients together and sprinkle a quarter of the mixture on to a flat dish or a baking tin that is not corrosive. Place the fish on the mixture, skin side down. Sprinkle half the mixture over the flesh, close up the fish and sprinkle the remainder on top.

3 Cover fish with two layers of kitchen foil and place a very heavy weight on top (perhaps a brick covered in a clean cloth).

4 Refrigerate for 3 days, turning the fish over once a day and basting with the liquor which will have formed.

Serving suggestion: Wipe the marinade off the fish and place on a wooden board. The fish should be cut in thin slanting slices and will have the texture of smoked salmon. Garnish with a little fresh dill if available. Serve with fresh bread and butter and a spicy mustard mayonnaise. Sauce Aioli is also a traditional accompaniment (*see* page 129).

Cream of Hot-Smoked Trout

Serves 6–8   Preparation time: 10 minutes   Cooking time: 25 minutes

A fish soup makes an uncommonly good starter. For this recipe you will need to have hot-smoked some of your own trout (*see* page 14), or you could purchase two small smoked trout.

225g/½lb hot-smoked trout flesh
  (bones and head reserved)
575ml/1 pint milk
tabasco
paprika
ground sea salt to taste
1 chopped onion
25g/1oz butter
1 teaspoon tomato purée
225g/½lb cooked potato
150ml/¼ pint double cream
chopped parsley for garnish

1 Place the bones and head of the fish in a pan with the milk and simmer for 20 minutes. Season with tabasco, salt and paprika. Strain and reserve stock.

2 Fry onion in butter until opaque.

3 Place the trout flesh, cooked onion, tomato purée, potato and half the milk in a blender and process, slowly pouring in remainder of milk.

4 Return the mixture to the pan, add cream and bring to simmering point. Do not boil. Taste and adjust seasoning and consistency as required.

Serving suggestion: Serve piping hot with a sprinkle of chopped parsley over each soup bowl, and with hot granary rolls.

CHAPTER 2

SUPPER DISHES

Panned Trout with Bacon

Serves 4   Preparation time: 20 minutes   Cooking time: 20 minutes

An easy and very tasty supper dish.

2 medium trout
2 rashers bacon
2 stalks celery
1 medium onion
½ green pepper
oil or bacon fat for frying
225ml/8fl oz dry white wine
salt and black pepper
chopped parsley and lemon slices

1 Gut, wash and dry the trout, removing heads and tails. Chop bacon and vegetables finely.

2 In a lidded pan or cast-iron casserole dish first fry the bacon then add vegetables and cook lightly. Place the trout over the bacon and vegetables.

3 Add the wine, cover with tight lid and cook over low heat for 15–20 minutes. Test with a fork, and if flesh parts easily from the bone, it is done.

4 To serve, place fish on a warm serving dish, and spoon over the vegetables and juices. Season with salt and grind black pepper over. Garnish with chopped parsley and lemon slices.

Serving suggestion: Serve with creamed potatoes and chopped cooked spinach.

Grilled Trout

Preparation time: 5 minutes   Cooking time: 6–10 minutes

Because of its delicate texture trout should never be placed closer to the grill than 10cm/4in. Many people enjoy eating the crispy skin whilst others will choose to remove it.

Allow a 225–250g/8–10oz trout per person.

Gut fish, cleaning skin and scraping out blood channel well. Leave the head and tail intact or remove as preferred. Pat fish dry. Score thick fish two or three time diagonally across the fleshiest parts to allow the heat to penetrate evenly. Season lightly with salt and pepper, and then brush with oil, bacon dripping or butter. Grill under maximum heat for 3–5 minutes per side, according to the thickness of the fish. Test with a fork to tell when the fish is cooked – if the flesh parts easily from the backbone, it is ready. Grilled trout can be served with brown bread and butter as a starter, with horseradish or tartare sauce, or as a main course with potatoes, green vegetables or salad.

Bacon dripping   Either for basting or frying, bacon dripping is an excellent alternative to butter and it will fry at a higher temperature without burning. Ask your butcher for bacon scraps, preferably a mixture of smoked and plain, and trim off any flesh which can be diced and fried for use in other recipes (such as Panned Trout with Bacon). Bake the pieces of fat in a hot oven (220°C/425°F/ Gas Mark 7) for approximately three-quarters of an hour and strain off fat which will keep for 3–4 weeks if covered and refrigerated.

Breakfast Trout

Preparation time: 10 minutes   Cooking time: 8–12 minutes

A creel full of small wild brown trout is ideal for this dish, a very special breakfast treat if you have been lucky enough to have had a good catch. You may also be able to buy small trout from your local trout farm.

Allow 3 fish per person and have 1 rasher of streaky bacon per fish.

Pre-heat the oven to 200°C/400°F/Gas Mark 6.

Clean and gut the trout, scraping out blood channel and removing heads. Pat the fish dry and wrap each in a rasher of streaky bacon. Place on a baking sheet and place in pre-heated oven until the bacon is crisp . Alternatively, grill both sides of the fish for 3–4 minutes, until the bacon is crisp. Serve with triangles of fried bread and baked fresh or tinned Italian tomatoes.

Hot Poached Trout

Preparation time: 5 minutes   Cooking time: 10–12 minutes

The tissues and fibres of trout are delicate, so treat the fish gently and season lightly, and remember that over-cooking dries out the flesh. As the length and thickness of a fish will be variable for a given weight the cooking time given is approximate, and you will need to check the flesh with the 'fork test'. Fundamentally, a short, thick fish of a given weight will take a little longer to cook than a longer, thinner fish of the same weight.

Allow approximately 200g/7oz per portion

Gut and wash the fish, preferably leaving the head on at this stage. Fill a fish kettle or long, deep baking dish with water, and season with salt and a liberal dash of vinegar. Bring to the boil and then immerse the fish (which need only just be covered by the liquid). When the liquid has returned to the boil, turn down to a very gentle simmer. To check when the fish is cooked, probe the thickest part by the backbone with a fork. If the flesh parts easily, it is ready.

Remove from the pan and skin the fish quickly, deciding whether or not to serve with the head on. Slide the fish on to a warm serving dish and garnish with Parsley Lemon Butter (*see* below). Serve with new potatoes and a favourite green vegetable such as asparagus or petits pois.

Parsley Lemon Butter

100g/4oz butter
1 tablespoon finely chopped
    parsley
2 teaspoons lemon juice
grated rind of 1 lemon
salt and pepper

Beat the butter until light and creamy. Fold in the parsley, lemon juice, grated rind, salt and pepper, and form the mixture into a long roll on greaseproof paper. Roll up in the paper, refrigerate until required, then cut into slices as a garnish.

Trout Baked in Foil

Serves 4   Preparation time: 8 minutes   Cooking time: 30 minutes

One of the simplest ways of cooking larger trout. The fish steam bakes and remains very moist.

1 large trout (say 700g/2lb)
25g/1oz butter
salt and pepper
a few fresh herbs as available
    (dill, tarragon, chervil,
    lovage)
lemon slices and watercress

Pre-heat the oven to 200°C/400°F/Gas Mark 6.

1   Gut and clean fish, scraping out blood channel well. Leave head on or off as desired. (Backbone and rib cage can be removed leaving head on – *see* filleting page 10). Dry fish inside and out with kitchen paper. Liberally season cavity, and place knobs of butter and any available herbs inside.

2   Enclose the fish in a loose but sealed foil parcel, place on a baking sheet and bake in the oven for 25–30 minutes.

3   Open parcel, skin fish quickly and slide on to warm serving dish. Garnish with watercress sprigs and lemon slices.

Serving suggestion: Boiled new potatoes, artichoke hearts and french beans.

Herb Baked Trout

Serves 6–8   Preparation time: 15 minutes   Cooking time: 40 minutes

This is an easy and flavoursome supper dish.

1 large trout

For the filling:
25g/1oz butter for frying
2–3 rashers streaky bacon
1 chopped onion
50g/2oz fresh breadcrumbs
pinch of sage
pinch of thyme
1 small egg, beaten
salt and pepper as required

Pre-heat the oven to 200°C/400°F/Gas Mark 6.

1 Gut and clean thoroughly, leaving head on. (Remove rib cage and backbone if desired – *see* page 10.) Fry the bacon and chop into pieces. Lightly fry the onions and add to the bacon with the breadcrumbs and herbs, and bind together with egg. (Alternatively you may use a package country stuffing mix as directed, adding the egg, bacon and onions.)

2 Fill the cavity of the fish with the filling. Place on kitchen foil and make a sealed parcel, leaving some air space within for steam to circulate. Bake in pre-set moderate oven for 20 minutes.

3 Uncover parcel and bake for a further 20 minutes. Remove from foil and place on a warm serving dish.

Serving suggestion: Leeks in white sauce and butterbeans.

Trout Poached in Stock and Cider

Serves 4   Preparation time: 5 minutes   Cooking time: 10 minutes

A succulent, savoury and simple dish.

4 average trout
272ml/½ pint cider (or white
wine)
Knorr fish stock cube
freshly ground black pepper
packet of savoury stuffing mix

1 Clean, gut and de-head trout. Put the fish in a deep pan and cover with wine or cider; dissolve in stock cube and season with black pepper. Bring to boiling point and simmer very gently for 5 minutes.

2 Sprinkle in the stuffing mix, turn down the heat until all is blended and absorbed when it will be ready to serve.

Serving suggestion: Crispy sauté potatoes and french beans.

Trout in Newspaper

Preparation time: 5 minutes   Cooking time: approximately 15 minutes

This is one of the most basic and effective ways of cooking a trout for an al fresco meal.

1 small trout per person

Pre-heat the oven to 200°C/400°F/Gas Mark 6.

1 Gut and thoroughly wash each trout, leaving head on or removing as required. Wrap each trout in a whole sheet of newspaper and wet thoroughly.

2 Place on a baking sheet in the oven for about 15 minutes or until the newspaper has fully dried out. Removing the paper will also conveniently remove the skin. Serve piping hot with buttery jacket potatoes.

Trout Fish Cakes

Serves 4   Preparation time: 15 minutes   Cooking time: 10 minutes

When you have a surplus of trout this makes an excellent basic meal. It is worth while making some extra for the freezer.

1 medium onion, chopped
2 rounds of bread soaked in milk
450g/1lb cooked trout flesh
   (poached or steamed)
2 teaspoons dried parsley
2 egg yolks
salt
paprika
2 tablespoons cooking oil
100g/4oz dried breadcrumbs for
   coating

1 Lightly fry chopped onion in oil. Squeeze moisture from bread, and then coarsely mix together the bread, fish, parsley and seasoning. Stir in egg yolks.

2 Heat the oil in a pan. Shape the mixture into flat cakes, press into dried breadcrumbs and then fry until golden-brown.

Serving suggestion: Broad beans in a white sauce, carrots and boiled potatoes.

Smoked Trout Fish Cakes

Serves 6–8   Preparation time: 15 minutes   Cooking time: 10 minutes

This dish presumes that you will have a batch of ready hot-smoked trout in the freezer. The alternative would be to purchase some. This would have the effect of making you realise just how cheaply you can produce your own!

675g/1½lb hot-smoked trout
1 large onion
2 tablespoons cooking oil
450g/1lb cold mashed potatoes
¼ cup chopped fresh parsley
salt and pepper
1 egg, beaten
2 tablespoons flour
50g/2oz dry breadcrumbs
parsley for garnish

1   Flake the fish well. Chop the onion and fry in a little oil until tender.

2   Combine the fish, potato, parsley and seasoning and mix together well. Shape into cakes, roll in flour, then egg and breadcrumbs, and fry in hot fat on each side until golden-brown. Garnish with parsley, and serve simply with tinned or fresh asparagus and bread and butter.

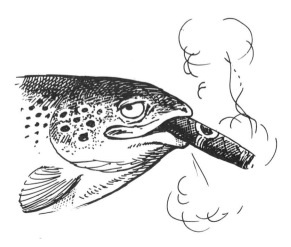

Troutie Leekie

Serves 4–6   Preparation time: 30 minutes   Cooking time: 30 minutes

A combination of baked trout and leeks in a white wine sauce.

4–6 medium trout
2–3 leeks, trimmed to mainly
white

For the sauce:
50g/2oz flour
50g/2oz butter
120ml/4fl oz dry white wine
150ml/¼ pint double cream
seasoning
100g/4oz dry breadcrumbs
50g/2oz strong grated cheese

Pre-heat the oven to 190°C/375°F/Gas Mark 5.

1   Gut and clean trout, removing heads. Boil leeks in salted water until just soft and cut each in half lengthwise. In a large casserole dish arrange leeks and trout alternately side by side. Cover with a lid and bake for 25 minutes.

2   For the sauce, fry the flour in the butter for 1 minute, slowly blend in the juices from the casserole dish, then add the white wine, cream and seasoning, stirring continuously until thickened. Pour back into casserole dish, sprinkle top with mixed breadcrumbs and grated cheese. Brown under grill.

3   Alternatively, add the juices around the fish to a tinned white wine sauce.

Serving suggestion: Duchesse potatoes and buttered minted carrots.

Trout and Egg Crumble

Serves 6–8   Preparation time: 20 minutes   Cooking time: 25 minutes

675g/1½lb ready-cooked trout
 flesh (either smoked or plain)
3 hard-boiled eggs
275ml/½pt made or packet
 cheese sauce

For the crumble topping:
40g/1½oz butter
75g/3oz flour
50g/2oz grated cheese
salt and pepper

Pre-heat the oven to 200°C/400°F/Gas Mark 6.

1 Flake flesh of trout roughly, removing any bones. Chop hard-boiled eggs, and then combine eggs and fish with the cheese sauce.

2 To make the topping, rub the butter and flour together until it resembles breadcrumbs; mix in the cheese and seasoning. Cover the fish mixture with the topping.

3 Bake for approximately 25 minutes until the top is browned.

Serving suggestion: Creamed potatoes and mixed diced vegetables.

Scandinavian Trout

Serves 4–6   Preparation time: 25 minutes   Cooking time: 30 minutes

This is a hot, savoury and crispy dish which makes an ideal al fresco meal.

4 average trout (say, 350g/12oz
  each)
1 tablespoon made mustard
1 tablespoon tomato purée
¹/₂ teaspoon sugar
2 tablespoons mayonnaise
knob of butter
salt and black pepper

Pre-heat the oven 190°C/375°F/Gas Mark 5.

1 Gut the fish, scrub the skin and fillet into individual halves (*see* page 10).

2 Mix all the ingredients (except butter) together and spread the mixture over the flesh side of each fillet. Roll fillets up, skin side out, and secure with cocktail sticks.

3 Arrange on a greased ovenproof dish, and dot with butter. Bake for 30 minutes until browned and crispy.

Serving suggestion: Serve with coleslaw, mixed salad and hot rolls.

Trout au Gratinée

Serves 4   Preparation time: 20 minutes   Cooking time: 8–10 minutes

Very simple and tasty.

2 trout, approximately 675g/
    1½lb each
2 tablespoons mayonnaise
100g/4oz grated cheese
salt
¼ teaspoon paprika

1 Gut, clean and fillet fish into four pieces. Pat dry with kitchen paper. Spread mayonnaise over flesh side of each fillet, and place them skin side down in a grill pan.

2 Sprinkle over grated cheese, salt and paprika, and place under hot grill until bubbly and brown.

Serving suggestion: Glazed minted carrots, chopped spinach, creamed potatoes.

Trout with Horseradish

Serves 4   Preparation time: 30 minutes   Cooking time: 20 minutes

A good supper dish which reheats well.

900g/2lb trout or 4 small trout
1 onion, sliced
1 carrot, sliced
1 stick celery, sliced
1 bay leaf
salt and freshly ground black
*   pepper*
2 tablespoons white vinegar

For the sauce:
25g/1oz flour
25g/1oz butter
½ cup fish stock (from cooking
*   the above ingredients)*
4 tablespoons single cream
½ teaspoon sugar
3 tablespoons creamed
*   horseradish*

1 Gut and fillet fish into four pieces, or gut, de-head and tail four smaller fish. Place vegetables and bay leaf in a large covered pan of salted water and simmer until tender. Strain vegetables, purée, and retain the liquor for stock.

2 Add vinegar to vegetable stock and poach the fish gently in this for about 10 minutes (test with a fork: if flesh parts easily it is done).

3 To make the sauce, fry the flour in the butter for 1 minute, gradually mix in the stock until thickened, and then add the sugar, vegetable purée and horseradish, stirring continuously. Remove from heat and stir in cream.

4 Transfer the fish to a warmed serving dish and pour over the sauce. Pasta shapes and broccoli spears would make an ideal accompaniment.

Note This dish could be pre-cooked and reheated in the oven under foil and served with piped creamed potato around the fish.

54

Trout Parmesan

Serves 4   Preparation time: 25 minutes   Cooking time: 30 minutes.

An Italian recipe which is useful when you have trout of various sizes which can be poached together.

450g/1lb cold poached trout flesh
25g/1oz butter
25g/1oz flour
125ml/4fl oz milk
50ml/2fl oz double cream
1 tablespoon made mustard
salt and pepper
2 tablespoons medium sherry
25g/1oz grated parmesan cheese
50g/2oz grated fresh
    breadcrumbs

Pre-heat the oven to 220°C/425°F/Gas Mark 7.

1 Have ready approximately 450g/1lb trout flesh from which skin and bones have been removed. Heat butter in a pan, blend in the flour and cook for 1 minute. Stir in the milk gradually, add the cream and mustard and stir until the sauce has thickened. Add seasoning and simmer for 5 minutes. Stir in the sherry and half the cheese.

2 Place fish in an ovenproof dish, pour the sauce over. Sprinkle with remaining cheese and breadcrumbs. Place in pre-heated oven and bake until browned on top.

Serving suggestion: Serve with stir-fry mixed vegetables and pasta twirls.

Open Sesame

Serves 4   Preparation time: 10 minutes   Cooking time: 10 minutes

This dish is particularly popular with children — being filleted the fish is easy to eat, and the cooked sesame seeds have a distinctive nutty taste.

2 large trout (say, 675g/1½lb
  each)
50g/2oz wholemeal flour
50g/2oz sesame seeds
1 teaspoon dried mixed herbs
salt and black pepper
1 beaten egg
25g/1oz butter
1 tablespoon cooking oil

1 Gut and clean trout, scrubbing skin well, and fillet out flat. Dry the fillets in kitchen paper, dust well with wholemeal flour.

2 Combine sesame seeds, herbs and seasoning. Dip the fillets in egg and coat thoroughly with the savoury seeds.

3 Put the butter and oil in a heavy frying pan and hot fry the fish, skin side first to prevent curling, until both sides are well browned.

Serving suggestion: Serve with a potato and cheese casserole and a fresh green vegetable.

Smoked Trout Chowder

Serves 6   Preparation time: 20 minutes   Cooking time: 20 minutes

This makes a good hearty supper dish. Preparation time presumes you have a supply of ready hot-smoked trout in your freezer store, otherwise smoked trout can be purchased from trout farms, freezer shops or delicatessens.

1 medium onion, sliced into rings
25g/1oz butter
675g/1½lb smoked trout
1 small tin Italian tomatoes,
   chopped
1 small tin sweet red peppers,
   chopped
1 tablespoon cornflour
275ml/½ pint milk
garlic salt
paprika

1 Fry onion in butter. Remove any bones and skin from fish, and flake.

2 Combine fish, tomatoes, peppers and onion in a pan and simmer for 15 minutes. Mix the flour into the milk and add slowly to fish mixture. Season. When thickened, simmer for a further 5 minutes.

Serving suggestion: Serve with plain boiled rice or pasta and a side salad.

Oven Crisp Trout

Serves 4   Preparation time: 20 minutes   Cooking time: 20 minutes

A quick and appetising dish. The skin of the fish will be brown and crispy.

4 portion-sized trout
salt and pepper
150g/5oz soft butter
2 tablespoons chopped parsley
2 eggs
1 tablespoon milk
freshly ground black pepper
100g/4oz dry breadcrumbs
100g/4oz finely grated Cheddar
 cheese

Pre-heat the oven to 200°C/400°F/Gas Mark 6.

1 Clean and gut trout leaving head and tail intact. Fillet out bones if desired (*see* page 10). Season with salt and pepper inside and out. Cream together butter and parsley and spread in cavity of fish.

2 Beat together eggs, milk, salt and pepper and dip trout in it. Combine the crumbs and cheese and roll the trout in this mixture. Place trout in a shallow buttered ovenproof dish and sprinkle any remaining crumb mixture on top. Dot with butter.

3 Bake trout in hot oven for 15–20 minutes and test with a fork to see when they are cooked. If flesh parts easily from backbone they are ready to be served.

Serving suggestion: Serve with creamed pototoes and braised celery.

Sour Cream Trout

Serves 4   Preparation time: 15 minutes   Cooking time: 30 minutes

4 medium trout (say, 275–350g/
*   10–12oz)*
275ml/¹/₂ pint soured cream
juice of half a lemon
1 teaspoon chopped chives
1 apple, finely grated
freshly ground white pepper
salt
50g/2oz fresh breadcrumbs

Pre-heat the oven to 200°C/400°F/Gas Mark 6.

1 Gut and clean trout, removing heads and tails. Mix all ingredients, except breadcrumbs, together to make the sauce.

2 Place the trout in an open casserole, pour the sauce over, sprinkle top with breadcrumbs and bake uncovered for 25–30 minutes.

Serving suggestion: Jerusalem artichokes and french beans would make pleasant accompaniments.

Trout and Shrimp Risotto

Serves 4   Preparation time: 20 minutes   Cooking time: 20–35 minutes

This makes an ideal fork supper. It becomes more of a party dish if smoked trout is used instead of poached trout.

225g/8oz flaked cooked trout
  flesh
50g/2oz butter
1 medium onion, chopped
175g/6oz long grain rice
1 red pepper, chopped
3 sticks of celery, chopped
1 large carrot, chopped
small tin of shrimps in brine
425ml/¾ pint water
pepper
chopped parsley

Pre-heat oven to 190°C/375°F/Gas Mark 5 (optional).

1 Have ready 225g/½lb flaked, poached or hot-smoked trout, free of bones and skin. In a lidded pan, melt butter and fry onion until opaque. Add rice and lightly toss over heat until all grains are oiled. Add the water, plus the brined water from the shrimps, and season with pepper. Add chopped vegetables and bring to the boil.

2 Simmer with the lid off until the liquid is almost absorbed. Add fish and shrimps. Turn the rice mixture occasionally to prevent sticking on the bottom of the pan and add a little more water if necessary. When the rice is just softened (about 20 minutes) it is ready to serve on its own with parsley sprinkled over.

3 Alternatively, bring the mixtture to the boil, add all ingredients and bake in pre-heated oven until all moisture is absorbed into the rice (about 35 minutes).

Crunchy Coated Trout

Serves 4   Preparation time: 25 minutes   Cooking time: 10 minutes

For those who love fish and chips, this is a special trouty version. The skin will be highly edible and crisp.

2 large trout (450–675g/1–1½lb)
25g/1oz flour
1 teaspoon onion salt
1 teaspoon dried mixed herbs
1 egg, beaten
75g/3oz muesli base (a mixture of
  jumbo flaked cereals)
oil for frying
lemon quarters and watercress

1 Gut, wash and fillet trout, removing all fins. Mix together flour, onion salt and herbs. Dry the fish on kitchen paper and roll in savoury flour. Dip in egg then coat well with the muesli mixture.

2 Fry each fish in hot oil, skin side first to prevent them curling, until they are well browned.

3 Place fillets on heated serving dish, top each with a lemon quarter and surround with watercress sprigs. Serve with chips and peas.

Trout Shepherd's Pie

Serves 4–6   Preparation time: 30 minutes   Cooking time: 25 minutes

An easy way to use up surplus trout in a fish pie — why not make two or three at a time and freeze.

1 stick celery, chopped
1 large carrot, chopped
50g/2oz butter
50g/2oz flour
425ml/³⁄₄ pint milk
1 teaspoon each of oregano,
 thyme and tarragon (or dried
 mixed herbs)
450g/1lb boned cooked trout
seasoning
450g/1lb cooked mashed potato

Pre-heat the oven to 200°F/400°C/Gas Mark 6.

1 Sauté vegetables in butter until soft. Add flour and stir in until blended. Cook for one minute, and then slowly stir in milk until a smooth sauce is formed. Add herbs, fish and seasoning as required.

2 Pile mixture into an ovenproof casserole. Pipe mashed potato over the top. Dot with butter and bake until golden brown on top.

An alternative quick method: For the sauce, substitute condensed asparagus or mushroom soup, adding 275ml/½ pint milk to dilute. Top with instant mashed potato.

Serving suggestion: A favourite green vegetable is all you need to complete this dish.

Smoked Trout Kedgeree

Serves 4   Preparation time: 10 minutes   Cooking time: 15 minutes

This is a very tasty supper dish. Preparation time assumes that you have home-smoked trout available, otherwise these may be purchased from some trout farms, delicatessens or freezer shops.

3 small hot-smoked trout
2 tablespoons olive oil
1 medium onion, sliced
4 heaped teaspoons patna rice
large pinch of curry powder
2 tablespoons sultanas
575ml/1 pint boiling water
salt and pepper
chopped parsley
2 hard-boiled eggs for garnish

1 Flake the trout, removing skin and bones.

2 Fry the onion in oil until pale golden. Stir in rice and coat all grains in oil. Add curry powder and sultanas. Pour in boiling water, and season with plenty of salt and a little pepper. Simmer gently with the lid off the pan, until most of the water is absorbed.

3 Add the fish, stirring gently from time to time to prevent sticking. Cook until rice is just soft.

Serving suggestion: Turn out on to individual plates and garnish with rough-chopped hard-boiled eggs and chopped parsley.

Trout and Pepper Flan

Serves 6   Preparation time: 30 minutes   Cooking time: 30 minutes

A spicy hot flan which can be made in advance and reheated.

225g/8oz shortcrust pastry
2 shallots, chopped
25g/1oz butter
225g/8oz hot-smoked trout flesh
1 small tin sweet red peppers
1 teaspoon curry powder
275ml/½ pint savoury white
    sauce (tinned, packet or home-
    made)
1 cup fresh breadcrumbs

Pre-heat the oven to 220°C/425°F/Gas Mark 7.

1 Line a 30cm/8in flan dish with shortcrust pastry and blind bake until biscuit-coloured.

2 Fry the chopped shallots in butter until soft. Mix into the white sauce, together with chopped red peppers, curry powder and fish.

3 Pour the filling into the flan case, cover with breadcrumbs and put back into the oven until browned on top.

Serving suggestion: Serve with hot jacket baked potatoes and runner beans.

Trout and Ham Lasagne

Serves 4   Preparation time: 20 minutes   Cooking time: 25 minutes

The trout and ham 'marry' together extremely well in this delicious dish.

2 trout (approx 400g/14oz each)
100g/4oz sliced cooked ham
ready-cooked lasagne slices
    (approx 6)
275ml/½ pint well-seasoned
    cheese sauce (packet, tinned
    or home-made)
25g/1oz Cheddar cheese, grated

Pre-heat the oven to 200°F/400°C/Gas Mark 6.

1 Fillet trout into 4 individual sides (*see* page 10).

2 Into a well-greased baking dish layer alternately half the ham, trout fillets, lasagne and cheese sauce in this order and then repeat layering with the other half. Sprinkle the grated cheese over the top of the final layer of cheese sauce.

3 Bake the lasagne in the pre-heated oven for approximately 25 minutes until well browned on top.

Serving suggestion: Creamed carrot and parsnip, runner beans.

Trout and Parsley Pie

Serves 4–6   Preparation time: 20 minutes   Cooking time: 35 minutes

A supper dish to make ahead of time and reheat as required.

1 good-sized trout (900g/2lb), or
*   two smaller fish*
275ml/½ pint milk for poaching
packet of white sauce or onion
*   sauce mix*
1 tablespoon chopped parsley
black pepper
2 hard-boiled eggs, chopped
350g/12oz cooked mashed potato
25g/1oz grated Cheddar cheese
paprika

Pre-heat the oven to 200°C/400°F/Gas Mark 6.

1   Gut and clean fish, removing head, and poach in milk for 10 minutes. Retain the milk, and remove the skin and bones from the fish.

2   Make up the packet sauce using the poaching milk, and add the fish, parsley, black pepper and chopped eggs to it.

3   Place in a baking dish. Decorate with piped mashed potato. Sprinkle the cheese over and dust with paprika. Bake for approximately 30 minutes, until brown on top.

Serving suggestion: Serve with baked tomatoes and a green vegetable.

Smoked Trout and Pasta Bake

Serves 4   Preparation time: 25 minutes   Cooking time: 30 minutes

A tasty fork supper dish, which calls upon your store of ready-smoked fish; otherwise, add preparation time for smoking from fresh, or purchase smoked trout.

225g/8oz pasta shells
1 medium onion, chopped
100g/4oz sliced fresh mushrooms
25g/1oz butter
1 small can sweetcorn, drained
1 tablespoon lemon juice
275ml/½ pint soured cream
100g/4oz strong cheese, grated
350g/12oz hot-smoked trout,
    flaked
black pepper, salt
chives or parsley, chopped

Pre-heat the oven to 190°C/375°F/Gas Mark 5.

---

1 Cook pasta shells, stir in a knob of butter after draining and keep warm.

---

2 Sauté onions, then mushrooms in the butter; when softened add the drained sweetcorn, lemon juice, soured cream, 75g/3oz grated cheese and flaked fish. Test for seasoning and adjust.

---

3 Combine pasta shells with the fish mixture. Pile into a casserole dish. Sprinkle the top with remaining grated cheese and bake for 25–30 minutes.

Serving suggestion: Serve into individual bowls and sprinkle fresh chives or parsley over each portion.

Smokey Trout with Green Noodles

Serves 4–6   Preparation time: 20 minutes   Cooking time: 20 minutes

This recipe assumes that you have hot-smoked trout stored in your freezer (*see* page 14). Alternatively, you may wish to purchase smoked trout.

350g/12oz flat green noodles
3 tablespoons olive oil
50g/2oz butter
1 large clove garlic, finely
  chopped
225g/8oz small button mushrooms
450g/1lb smoked trout, flaked
2 egg yolks
1 tablespoon tomato purée
275ml/½ pint single cream
salt and black pepper
parsley

1 In a large lidded saucepan bring salted water to the boil, add noodles and boil for 11–12 minutes, stirring initially to separate. When just soft, drain and place in a warmed serving dish; mix in a tablespoon of olive oil and keep warm in a low oven.

2 In a large deep frying pan melt the butter with the remaining olive oil, add chopped garlic and fry until tender. Add mushrooms (sliced in half if they are not very small), cook until just softened, and then add flaked trout.

3 Whisk egg yolks and tomato purée into the cream and pour mixture slowly into frying pan. Stir to heat through and thicken without boiling, and then allow to simmer for about 5 minutes. Season with salt and pepper to taste. Pour mixture over the noodles, sprinkle with parsley, and serve on its own or with a side salad.

Trout and Tuna Macaroni

Serves 4   Preparation time: 15 minutes   Cooking time: 15 minutes

It is a great temptation to rush back from fishing, gut your trout and pop them into the freezer. Why not toss a couple into boiling water – they will then keep for several days in the fridge. This is one of many recipes using ready-poached trout.

225g/8oz macaroni
50g/2oz butter
1 large onion, chopped into rings
50g/2oz flour
425ml/³⁄₄ pint warmed milk
1 small tin tuna in brine, drained
350g/12oz poached trout flesh
150g/4oz grated cheese
salt and pepper
50g/2oz fresh breadcrumbs

1 Sprinkle the macaroni into a large pan of well-salted, fast-boiling water. Stir to separate pieces and boil gently for 8–10 minutes until tender. Drain and place in a lidded ovenproof dish with a knob of butter; cover and keep warm.

2 Melt butter in frying pan, add onion and fry until tender. Blend in flour and cook for 1 minute. Add milk gradually, stirring continuously for 4 minutes. Add the tuna and trout flesh, and stir until heated through, breaking trout up into bite-sized pieces. Stir in grated cheese. Season to taste.

3 Combine with the macaroni, sprinkle breadcrumbs on top and brown under a hot grill. Serve at once on its own or with a side salad.

Fresh Pasta with Smoked Trout Sauce

Serves 4   Preparation time: 1 hour   Cooking time: 5 minutes

A good pasta that is well cooked is a pleasure to eat, and is also surprisingly high in protein content. The most popular shapes are thin noodles, spaghetti, tagliatelle, spirals, rings, shells, macaroni and coloured versions flavoured with spinach or tomato.

225g/8oz cold-smoked trout, or
  smoked salmon off-cuts
250ml/½ pint double cream
1 tablespoon dill seeds
pinch of paprika
3 tablespoons olive oil
parsley to garnish
500g/1lb preferred pasta shapes
  (fresh if available)
salt

1 Cut the fish into thin strips, removing any skin and bones. Put the cream in a bowl and beat lightly, and then add the fish. Leave to infuse for 1 hour – the cream will take on the flavour of the smoked trout.

2 Bring plenty of water to the boil and add 2 tablespoons salt. Add a dash of the oil to the water (to prevent pasta sticking together), and cook the pasta shapes. Fresh pasta needs from as little as 30 seconds to 3 minutes to cook according to thickness. It is perfect when it is slightly firm to eat, or *al dente*. Drain and keep warm.

3 Add remaining olive oil and other ingredients to the cream and fish, warm through gently but do not boil. Pour over pasta in serving dish.

Serving suggestion: Garnish with fresh parsley and serve with a side salad.

Trout Treat

Serves 2   Preparation time: 25 minutes   Cooking time: 15 minutes

A little luxury dish for two when you feel like a special supper.

2 small smoked trout
25g/1oz butter
1 tablespoon flour
¼ cup chicken or fish stock
(made from a cube)
½ cup milk
black pepper
1 tablespoon strong cheese,
grated
2 teaspoons sherry
4 cups cooked rice (kept hot)
1 tin asparagus tips, warmed

1 Flake the trout into large pieces. Melt the butter in a pan and add the flour, stirring for a minute. Gradually blend in the stock and milk, and season with pepper. Boil for 5 minutes, stirring to prevent sticking.

2 Blend in cheese and sherry, add fish and warm through.

Serving suggestion: Pile hot rice in the centre of each plate, make a well in the rice and fill with the mixture. Surround with asparagus.

Smoked Trout and Potato Casserole

Serves 4   Preparation time: 15 minutes   Cooking time: 1 hour

This is a good standby dish in a luxury class. It can be made some days in advance and it freezes well.

3 large old potatoes
175g/6oz cold-smoked trout,
  sliced (or smoked salmon)
175g/6oz fried bacon, chopped
black pepper and salt
150ml/¼ pint double cream
275ml/½ pint milk
50g/2oz grated cheese

Pre-heat the oven to 190°C/375°F/Gas Mark 5.

1 Grease the bottom of a deep casserole.

2 Slice potatoes very finely (best done in a food processor), and put a layer of potatoes on the bottom of the dish. Season. Put in a layer of fish, a layer of potatoes, a layer of bacon and so on until all is used up and well seasoned, ending with a layer of potato slices.

3 Mix the cream and milk together and pour into the casserole. Top casserole with grated cheese.

4 Cover and bake for half an hour. Uncover and cook for a further 25–30 minutes until potatoes are soft and the top of the dish is browned.

Serving suggestion: Serve on its own as a fork supper, or with a green vegetable.

Note Assemble the ingredients as quickly as possible otherwise the potatoes will discolour. Baking time will vary according to the variety of potato.

CHAPTER 3

PARTY DISHES

Trout Grand Marnier

Serves 4   Preparation time: 15 minutes   Cooking time: 15 minutes

A simple to make main course which is a bit of a luxury.

4 fresh trout (350g/12oz each)
50g/2oz butter
200ml/7fl oz double cream
2 tablespoons Grand Marnier
2 tablespoons Cognac
sea salt and freshly ground
    pepper
50g/2oz toasted almond flakes

1 Gut and clean the trout, leaving heads on. Melt butter in a thick-bottomed frying pan and sauté trout gently for about 5 minutes each side, testing with a fork to see if flesh parts easily from the backbone. Place trout on heated serving dish, cover and keep warm.

2 Add cream to the pan and warm through. Stir in the Grand Marnier and Cognac and season to taste. Pour the sauce over the trout and sprinkle toasted almond slices over.

Serving suggestion: Serve with tiny new potatoes, fresh asparagus and celery hearts.

Trout Berlin

Serves 4–6   Preparation time: 30 minutes   Cooking time: 15 minutes

A traditional recipe for round fish, which adapts well with trout. Being filleted, the fish is very easy to eat.

4–6 even-sized trout
seasoned flour for dusting skins
175g/6oz butter
orange slices for garnish
25g/1oz caster sugar
juice of 1 lemon and 1 orange
1 tablespoon parsley, chopped

For the filling:
4 shallots
100g/4oz button mushrooms
100g/4oz cooked spinach
mixed herbs
salt and pepper

1 Clean and fillet trout – leaving heads and tails on (*see* page 10). Dust the trout skins with seasoned flour.

2 To prepare the filling, finely chop the shallots and soften in 50g/2oz butter. Chop mushrooms and cook lightly, and then add spinach and seasoning. Allow filling to cool.

3 Stuff fish with filling and reshape. Place a knob of butter in a flameproof casserole, put in the trout and sauté underside of fish for 5 minutes.

4 Place casserole dish under hot grill to complete cooking and to brown top sides of fish (approximately 8 minutes).

5 In a separate pan melt remaining butter. Dust orange slices with caster sugar and fry until they turn brown – reserve for garnish. Pour orange and lemon juice into pan and heat through. Pour the juices over the trout and garnish with orange slices and parsley.

Serving suggestion: Serve with crisp sauté potatoes and Chinese leaves.

Trout Wellington

Serves 6–8   Preparation time: 30 minutes   Cooking time: 35 minutes

This is an impressive party dish, certain to produce gasps of admiration.

1 large trout (900g–1.4kg/2½–
*   3lb)*
1 medium onion, chopped
225g/8oz mushrooms, chopped
50g/2oz butter
50g/2oz fresh white breadcrumbs
salt and black pepper
225g/8oz shortcrust pastry
1 egg yolk for glaze
watercress and lemon wedges for
*   garnish*

Pre-heat the oven to 220°C/425°F/Gas Mark 7.

1   Wash, gut and fillet trout, keeping the two halves joined by the skin (*see* page 10); pat dry. Fry the onions and mushrooms in butter, toss in the breadcrumbs and brown slightly. Season the fillets and filling with salt and pepper.

2   Roll out pastry into an oblong slightly larger than the two fillets. Pack the trout with filling and re-assemble fillets to whole fish shape. Encase the fish in pastry. Slit top surface in two or three places to allow the steam to escape. Decorate top with spare pieces of pastry in little mushroom shapes or leaf shapes. Brush top with egg yolk.

3   Bake for 10 minutes in pre-heated oven, then reduce to moderate heat (190°C/375°F/Gas Mark 5) and cook for a further 20–25 minutes. Transfer to a warmed serving dish and garnish with watercress and lemon wedges.

Serving suggestion: Serve with creamed potatoes and a selection of lightly-coooked vegetables.

Trout Provençal

Serves 4   Preparation time: 20 minutes   Cooking time: 25 minutes

This is an adaptation of a traditional French recipe. For the hostess in a hurry a good Provençal sauce can be purchased in a tin.

2 large trout (450–675g/1–1½lb
  each)
1 tablespoon vinegar
1 tablespoon salt
water to cover fish

For the sauce:

1 tablespoon cooking oil
1 medium onion, chopped
1 clove garlic, crushed
100g/4oz mushrooms, chopped
150ml/¼ pint fish or chicken
  stock
150ml/¼ pint white wine
2 tinned sweet red peppers,
  chopped small

10oz peeled tomatoes, chopped
1 teaspoon sugar
2 teaspoons tomato purée
1 bay leaf
1 teaspoon parsley, chopped
1 teaspoon fresh marjoram, basil
  or tarragon as available
seasoning
stuffed olives for garnish

1 Gut and clean the fish, leaving heads on. Bones can be removed if required (*see* page 10). In a fish kettle or long baking dish bring water, vinegar and salt to the boil, immerse trout and simmer for 10 minutes. Turn off heat.

2 To make the sauce, heat oil in frying pan, add onion, garlic and mushrooms and toss until soft. Add the stock, wine, peppers, sugar, tomatoes, purée, bay leaf, herbs and seasoning. Simmer uncovered for 10 minutes. Discard bay leaf.

3 Remove fish fillets from bones if necessary and skin carefully. Lay on a warmed serving platter, pour the sauce over and garnish with sliced stuffed olives.

Serving suggestion: Serve with a plain boiled rice.

Trout Tahitian Style

Serves 2   Preparation time: 20 minutes   Marinating time: 4 hours

A traditional way of serving trout in Tahiti. Coconut cream adds an exotic flavour and is well worth seeking out from speciality shops.

4 fillets trout
juice of 1½ lemons (for
*   marinating)*
1 medium onion, finely chopped
2 tomatoes, cubed
2 tablespoons chives, chopped
50ml/2 fl oz coconut cream
juice of ½ lemon (for dressing)
seasoning

1 Place the fillets in a shallow dish and drizzle over with the lemon juice. Leave for 4 hours to marinate, then drain and discard liquid.

2 Cut the fish into thin strips and toss gently with the onion, tomatoes and chives.

3 Make a dressing of the coconut cream and lemon juice and spoon over the fish mixture. Season well.

Serving suggestion: Serve in shell dishes for maximum effect.

Trout Seville

Serves 6   Preparation time: 20 minutes   Cooking time: 15 minutes

Seville oranges are only available in January and February and are used for marmalade-making. If you like this recipe, it would be worth saving a few oranges in the freezer; alternatively, you could use two sweet oranges and one lemon.

6 portion-sized trout
3 Seville oranges
25g/1oz flour
75g/3oz butter
1 tablespoon cooking oil
25g/1oz cornflour
salt and black pepper
6 sweet orange slices for garnish
12 mint leaves for garnish

1 Wash and gut fish, leaving heads on. Pat dry. Slash each side three times at thickest part.

2 Finely grate rind from one orange and squeeze the juice from all three. Pour a little juice into each cut of the fish and moisten skins with juice. Dust skins with flour.

3 Heat half the butter and oil in a frying pan and fry the trout until crisp and golden. Remove from the pan and keep warm on a serving dish.

4 Heat the rest of the butter. Mix cornflour to a paste with orange juice, and add to the pan with the remainder of the juice. Stir until thickened and adjust with water to make a sauce of pouring consistency. Add grated rind, salt and black pepper.

5 Spoon the sauce over the fish. Garnish each fish with a fresh orange slice and two mint leaves.

Serving suggestion: Serve with creamed potatoes and broad beans in a white sauce.

Oriental Trout

Serves 4   Preparation time: 20 minutes   Cooking time: 40 minutes

This dish is modified from an Indonesian recipe and could form part of a meal with a Chinese theme. It can be prepared a day in advance and benefits from marinating overnight.

4 portion-sized trout
100g/4oz dessicated coconut
150ml/¼ pint hot water, lightly
*   salted*
2.5cm/1in piece of fresh ginger,
*   peeled and crushed*
1 tablespoon chopped dill
juice of one lime
¼ teaspoon lemon pepper or fish
*   seasoning*

1 Gut and clean fish well, leaving head on. Make three incisions with a sharp knife through thickest part on each side.

2 Soak dessicated coconut in hot water and leave to cool, and then stir in ginger, chopped dill, lime juice and seasoning. Put the fish into a lidded baking dish. Arrange mixture over fish, refrigerate, and leave for 6 hours, or overnight, to marinate.

Pre-heat the oven to 180°F/350°C/Gas Mark 4.

3 Bake covered for 40 minutes.

Serving suggestion: Serve with Chinese noodles, water chestnuts and crispy mange-tout peas.

Trout Ratatouille

Serves 4   Preparation time: 25 minutes   Cooking time: 30 minutes

1 large (900g/2lb) or 4 small
  (225g/8oz) trout
4 tablespoons vegetable oil
1 green pepper, chopped
2 large onions, chopped
4 courgettes, sliced crosswise
450g/1lb skinned tomatoes, or
  large tin Italian tomatoes
3 tablespoons tomato purée
1 teaspoon fresh dill, chopped
garlic salt
chilli pepper
juice ½ lemon
2 teaspoons arrowroot (optional)

1 Clean and fillet a large trout (*see* page 10), dividing it into four, or clean and de-head four trout.

2 Heat oil in a large lidded pan, add chopped green pepper, onions and courgette slices and fry until soft. Add the tomatoes, tomato purée, dill and seasoning. Cover and cook for 15 minutes.

3 Place fish in with the vegetable sauce, add lemon juice, cover and cook over a low heat for a further 15 minutes. Thicken juices with arrowroot if desired.

Serving suggestion: Serve on a bed of rice with a green side salad.

Buttered Trout with Almonds

Serves 4   Preparation time: 20 minutes   Cooking time: 15 minutes

Probably the best-known way of serving trout, especially popular in restaurants.

4 trout
75g/3oz butter
dash of cooking oil
30g/2oz flaked almonds
juice of 1 lemon
freshly ground salt and black
*   pepper*
watercress to garnish

1 Gut the trout, leaving the heads on. Wipe the fish dry with kitchen paper and season all over with salt and pepper.

2 Heat 25g/1oz butter in a heavy frying pan with a dash of oil. When foaming place the trout in the pan and fry on both sides for about 5 minutes each. Test with a fork: if flesh parts easily from backbone it is done. Remove fish to a warm serving dish.

3 Melt remaining butter in frying pan. Fry the almonds until golden-brown and stir in the lemon juice. When heated through pour over the trout. Garnish around dish with sprigs of watercress.

Serving suggestion: Serve with tiny new potatoes and braised celery.

Smoked Trout and Prawn Mornay

Serves 6   Preparation time: 25 minutes   Cooking time: 30 minutes

This recipe presumes that you have some hot-smoked trout in your freezer store. Add additional preparation time if smoking from fresh, or purchase ready-smoked fish.

3 medium hot-smoked trout
2 shallots, chopped
25g/1oz butter
175g/6oz frozen prawns, peeled
275ml/1/2 pint made white sauce
    (packet, tinned or home-
    made)
50g/2oz strong grated cheese
225g/8oz creamed potato

Pre-heat the oven to 200°C/400°F/Gas Mark 6.

1   Carefully remove heads, skin and bones from fish.

2   Lightly sauté the shallots in butter. Lay the smoked fish fillets in a shallow casserole dish and sprinkle over the shallots and prawns.

3   Stir most of the cheese into the white sauce, and pour over the fish. Pipe decoratively with creamed potato rosettes. Sprinkle remainder of cheese over the top.

4   Bake in a moderate oven for 30 minutes.

Serving suggestion: Serve with plain boiled rice, glazed minted carrots and braised celery.

Note This can be easily be made in advance and baked when required.

Honeyed Trout

Serves 6   Preparation time: 20 minutes   Cooking time: 45 minutes

This recipe was inspired by a West Indian fish dish.

6 trout (250–300g/9–11oz)
2 onions, finely sliced
100g/4oz mushrooms, finely sliced
1 teaspoon ground cumin
2 tablespoons clear honey
2 tablespoons water
120ml/4fl oz white wine
salt and pepper

1 Gut and wash the fish, removing heads. Pat dry with kitchen paper. Arrange in a shallow ovenproof dish. Scatter the onions, mushrooms and cumin on top.

2 Heat the honey in a saucepan over a low heat, add water, wine, and salt and pepper to taste. Pour marinade over fish, cover and leave in a cool place for 1 hour for the juices to be absorbed into the fish.

Pre-heat the oven to 170°C/325°F/Gas Mark 3.

3 Bake covered with aluminium foil for 45 minutes.

Serving suggestion: Serve with hot pineapple slices, boiled new potatoes and broccoli spears.

Coloubiac

Serves 4–6   Preparation time: 30 minutes   Cooking time: 40 minutes

Trout in a savoury sauce in a golden puff pastry case.

1 large trout, filleted and skinned
575ml/1 pint milk
1 medium onion, chopped
50g/2oz butter
50g/2oz flour
1 Knorr fish stock cube
100g/4oz cooked rice
120g/4½oz can sliced mushrooms
1 tablespoon chopped parsley
350g/12oz puff pastry
1 beaten egg

Pre-heat the oven to 220°F/425°F/Gas Mark 7.

1 Poach the trout fillets in milk for 5 minutes. Remove trout and reserve the milk.

2 In a saucepan, sauté onion in butter until tender. Add flour and stir for one minute. Gradually add milk and stock cube, and cook for 2 minutes until thick and bubbly.

3 Break the fish into pieces and put into sauce, together with the rice, mushrooms, parsley and seasoning. Stir to mix evenly. Allow to cool.

4 Roll pastry out into a rectangle, 50×20cm (20×10in). Pile fish mixture down the centre of the pastry. Fold up and seal contents, moistening edges with egg yolk, and transfer whole gently to a greased baking sheet, turning seam side down. Allow to rest for half an hour in a cool place.

5 Bake for 15 minutes at pre-set heat. Turn oven down slightly and continue to bake for approximately 25 minutes until pastry is puffed and golden. Carefully slide on to a serving plate.

Serving suggestion: Slice to serve with sour cream and chives as a sauce. Accompany with a mixed dressed salad.

Poached Trout with Fennel

Serves 2   Preparation time: 20 minutes   Cooking time: 2½ hours

In appearance fennel closely resembles dill but has a sweet anise flavour that is altogether different. It is well known as a fish herb.

2 fresh trout (225g/8oz each)
1 small head fennel (175g/6oz)
350g/12oz potatoes
1 bay leaf
50ml/2fl oz dry vermouth
Seasoning
25g/1oz butter

1 Clean the trout, leaving the head and tail intact. Wash well. Trim the leaves from the fennel and reserve. Thinly slice the fennel. Peel and slice the potato thinly. Arrange the vegetables in a slow cooker with the bay leaf.

2 Pour over the vermouth and 50ml/2fl oz water. Season well. Place the trout over the fennel and potato and dot with butter.

3 Cover and cook on 'High' for 2½ hours. Garnish with the reserved finely chopped fennel leaves.

Serving suggestion: Serve with buttered carrots and broad beans.

Trout Sweet and Sour

Serves 4   Preparation time: 20 minutes   Cooking time: 20 minutes

Based on the traditional Chinese recipe. The pungent flavour will disguise the occasional shortcomings of very early or late season fish which are not in the best of condition.

2 large trout

For the sauce:
50g/2oz flour
oil for frying
225ml/8fl oz water
125ml/4fl oz vinegar
75g/3oz sugar
2 teaspoons tomato purée
2 teaspoons cornflour
1 tablespoon soy sauce
½ teaspoon paprika

1 First prepare the sauce by bringing water, vinegar, sugar and tomato purée to the boil in a saucepan.

2 Blend cornflour to a paste with a little water and add to the pan together with soy sauce and paprika. Stir until thickened.

3 Gut and clean the fish well, removing heads. Make three diagonal cuts on each side and roll the fish in flour, coating thoroughly.

4 Heat oil in a large heavy pan. Hold the fish over and baste the cuts with hot oil, then put the fish into the oil and fry until browned on each side. Test to see if flesh parts easily from the backbone when it will be ready to serve.

5 Place on a heated dish. Pour a little of the sauce over and serve remainder in a sauce-boat.

Serving suggestion: Noodles and crisp mange-tout peas.

Trout in White Wine

Serves 4   Preparation time: 10 minutes   Cooking time: 20 minutes

This is a simple party dish which the hostess can prepare early on and reheat very gently under foil.

4 medium trout
275ml/½ pint white wine
salt and black pepper
40g/1½oz butter
1 tablespoon flour
1 tablespoon lemon juice
1 egg yolk
15g/¼oz fresh milled parsley

1 Clean and gut the fish, removing heads. Season with salt and pepper and place in a covered dish with the white wine. Simmer gently for about 10 minutes until cooked, and test with a fork to see if the flesh parts easily, when it will be done. Remove fish from the pan and keep warm, retaining juices.

2 Melt butter in a small pan, add flour and cook gently for 1 minute. Blend in the juices in which the fish were poached, stir constantly until the sauce thickens, and add lemon juice.

3 Finally, blend a little hot sauce with the egg yolk, remove sauce from heat and blend the egg yolk mixture into it. Place fish on warmed serving dish and pour the sauce over.

Serving suggestion: Serve with creamed potatoes and broad beans.

Trout Stuffed with White Fish

Serves 6   Preparation time: 40 minutes   Cooking time: 35 minutes

*6 medium trout (filleted, see page
    10)*
2 shallots, finely chopped
40g/1½oz butter
125ml/4fl oz white wine
1 tablespoon brandy
1 tablespoon chopped parsley
few sprigs of watercress

For the stuffing:
*450g/1lb white fish (cod, whiting,
    etc)*
3 egg whites
200ml/7oz carton double cream
seasoning

Pre-heat the oven to 200°C/400°F/Gas Mark 6.

1 Remove all skin and bones from white fish, place with egg whites, cream and
    seasoning in blender and process for 30 seconds.

2 Spread the mixture into each trout fillet and reshape fish. Place carefully into
    a well-greased lidded ovenproof dish. Bake in pre-set oven for 30 minutes.

3 Meanwhile, soften the shallots in butter, add wine and seasoning, cook
    rapidly for one minute, and then add brandy and parsley. Place the trout on a
    warmed serving dish and pour sauce over. Garnish with watercress.

Serving suggestion: Serve with sauté potatoes, braised celery and calabrese.

Trout with Hazelnuts and Grapes

Serves 6   Preparation time: 25 minutes   Cooking time: 15 minutes

An abundance of hazelnuts in the hedgerows in the autumn inspired this recipe; at the same time of year grapes are inexpensive.

about 2 dozen hazelnuts
6 portion-sized trout
50g/2oz plain flour
salt and black pepper
50g/2oz butter
150ml/¼ pint double cream or
*   yoghurt*
175g/6oz seedless green grapes

1 Shell hazelnuts, simmer in boiling water for 5 minutes, drain and, when cool enough to handle, slice in half.

2 Gut and clean trout, leaving heads on. Dry with kitchen paper. Season flour with salt and pepper and roll each trout in the seasoned flour.

3 In a heavy pan, melt enough butter to cover the base. Heat. When it stops foaming add the trout, and cook on each side until golden-brown. Remove trout to a heated dish and keep warm while making sauce.

4 Discard any butter left in pan and wipe clean with kitchen paper. Return pan to heat and add remaining butter. Fry the sliced hazelnuts until brown, tossing them so they do not burn. Remove nuts to a piece of kitchen paper until required. Pour cream or yoghurt into pan, increase the heat, bubble and reduce liquid by half. Halve and add grapes until warmed through. Taste and adjust seasoning.

5 Pour sauce over the trout and scatter the hazelnuts over.

Serving suggestion: Serve with sauté potatoes and french beans; or try braised lettuce (*see* page 135), as there is often a surplus in the kitchen garden in the autumn.

Trout Quenelles

Serves 4   Preparation time: 1 hour 25 minutes   Cooking time: 15 minutes

This traditional French dish is often made with pike, a coarse fish which is not to everyone's taste. This version is, in my opinion, much more refined. The dish can be made a day in advance and reheated but you must keep the quenelles and the sauce separate until final preparation.

225g/8oz filleted trout flesh
150ml/¼ pint double cream
1 egg
salt and paprika
pinch of grated nutmeg
100g/4oz peeled shrimps

For the sauce:
25g/1oz butter
1 tablespoon plain flour
300ml/½ pint milk
50g/2oz grated Gruyère cheese
seasoning
parsley, chopped

---

1 Put the fish, cream, egg, salt, paprika and nutmeg into a food processer and blend for 30 seconds. Transfer mixture to a bowl and refrigerate for ½ hour. Roll mixture into a long sausage 2cm/¾in round on a floured board and cut into 5cm/2in lengths.

---

2 Fill a saucepan with water. Bring to the boil. Drop fish pieces into water a few at a time – they will be cooked when they rise to the surface. Drain and place on kitchen paper.

---

3 Arrange on a buttered ovenproof dish with the shrimps, cover with foil and keep warm.

---

4 To make the sauce, melt butter in a saucepan, add flour and cook for 1 minute. Gradually add milk, stirring constantly, then add half the cheese, season, stir and simmer for 1 minute. Pour the sauce over the quenelles and sprinkle remaining cheese on top. Brown under hot grill. Garnish with parsley and serve as an entrée with brown bread and butter.

Braised Trout in Cider

Serves 4   Preparation time: 30 minutes   Cooking time: 30 minutes

This was originally a French recipe for trout cooked in champagne, which seemed a little extravagant. I have tried it using a dry cider, which I imagine is even tastier than using bubbly!

4 trout (275g/10oz each)
1 medium carrot
1 medium onion
2 stalks celery
2 shallots
50g/2oz butter
large lettuce leaves
1 cup dry cider
3 tablespoons double cream
salt and pepper

Pre-heat the oven to 200°C/400°F/Gas Mark 6.

1 Gut and wash trout leaving heads on. Dry with kitchen paper and season cavity.

2 Finely cut vegetables into strips and sauté in one-third of the butter. Fill the cavities of the trout with vegetables.

3 Dip individual lettuce leaves into boiling water for a couple of seconds to blanch them and make them pliable. Wrap each trout in one or two leaves to cover them completely. Place trout in buttered baking dish. Dot with the rest of the butter, pour cider over and place in pre-heated oven for 20 minutes, basting occasionally.

4 Stir in the cream and continue to bake for a further 10 minutes.

Serving suggestion: Serve hot from the baking dish with buttered noodles and spoon sauce over each portion.

Trout Grenobloise

Serves 4–6   Preparation time: 20 minutes   Cooking time: 30 minutes

Cold casserole-baked trout with a distinctive creamy dressing.

4–6 even-sized trout
275ml/½ pint water
2 lemons
6 peppercorns
1 onion, sliced

For the dressing:
1 dessertspoon creamed
  horseradish sauce
2–3 tablespoons dry sherry
4 tablespoons whipped cream
salt, pepper and sugar to taste
chopped parsley for garnish

Pre-heat the oven to 190°C/375°F/Gas Mark 5.

---

1 Clean and gut trout leaving heads and tails on (*see* page 10). Place in a casserole dish with water, juice of 1 lemon, peppercorns and onion. Place casserole in pre-heated oven for 30 minutes. Leave trout to cool in the liquid.

---

2 Carefully skin fish, leaving heads on, and arrange on a serving dish. Cover with clear film and refrigerate.

---

3 Grate the rind of 1 lemon and reserve zest for garnish. Peel the other lemon and cut into segments.

---

4 Into a bowl put lemon segments, horseradish, sherry, whipped cream and seasoning (including a little sugar), mix carefully, taste and adjust seasoning as required. Spoon sauce over each fish, scatter lemon zest and parsley over.

Serving suggestion: Serve with endive and watercress salad, small beetroot and brown bread and butter.

Trout in Parcels

Serves 4   Preparation time: 25 minutes   Cooking time: 20 minutes

This makes a very special dinner party dish, and the filleted fish make it very easy for guests who cannot cope with bones.

4 trout (350–400g/12–14oz)
225g/8oz shaped pasta
1 medium carrot
1 medium leek
1 small fennel (optional)
100g/4oz large white mushrooms
50g/2oz butter
125ml/4fl oz white wine
275ml/½ pint white sauce (home-
  made, packet or tinned)

Pre-heat the oven to 200°C/400°F/Gas Mark 6.

1 Wash and fillet trout (*see* page 10), leaving halves joined. Cook pasta, stir in a good knob of butter and keep warm.

2 Cut all the vegetables into thin strips. Put remaining butter in a pan with a lid, add the vegetables and cook slowly with lid on until just soft.

3 Have ready four large pieces of kitchen foil. Put a layer of vegetables on a piece of foil, then the fish, a few vegetables between the fillets, then a few on top. Pull up the sides of the foil, pour in a quarter of the white wine and seal the parcel well, leaving some space within to allow steam to circulate. Bake in a moderate oven for 20 minutes.

4 Remove from heat. Open a corner to pour out juices, add these to the ready-made sauce, taste and adjust seasoning if necessary. Pour the sauce over the pasta and serve with the fish, with perhaps runner beans or peas as accompaniment.

Marinated Trout

Serves 4   Preparation time: 20 minutes (plus overnight marinating)   Cooking time: 25 minutes

This dish needs to be prepared the day before and is then quick and simple for a busy hostess to produce.

2 trout (900g/2lb each)
1 onion, thinly sliced
1 lemon, thinly sliced
1 clove garlic, crushed
salt and pepper
1 dessertspoon olive oil
175ml/6fl oz dry white wine or
    cider
2 tablespoons thick cream

---

1   Fillet trout out into four individual pieces (*see* page 10). Oil the base of an ovenproof dish and lay in the trout fillets, with the onion and lemon slices on top. Sprinkle with garlic, salt and pepper. Pour over oil and wine or cider, cover with foil, and place in fridge to marinate overnight.

Pre-heat the oven to 200°C/400°F/Gas Mark 6.

2   Place the covered ovenproof dish in the oven and bake for 25 minutes. Stir in the cream just before serving.

Serving suggestion: Suitable accompaniments would be creamed potatoes and petits pois.

Truite au Bleu

Serves 1 or 2 per trout, according to size   Preparation time: 5 minutes   Cooking time: 5 minutes

A traditional recipe for the freshest of freshly-caught trout that are not over 450g/1lb in weight.

trout
vinegar
fish stock cube

1 Gut and clean fish, scraping blood channel out under running cold water. Place the required number of fish in a deep pan. Pour over 125ml/4fl oz vinegar, cover with water which has been well seasoned with a fish stock cube, and bring to the boil.

2 Remove from heat and, keeping tightly covered, allow to stand for 5 minutes.

Serving suggestion: Serve with a Hollandaise sauce and a selection of lightly-cooked fresh vegetables.

Trout Baked with Prawns

Serves 4–6 according to size of fish   Preparation time: 15 minutes   Cooking time: 30 minutes

A luxury dinner party dish.

2 medium or 1 large trout
175g/6oz shelled prawns
275ml/½ pint white sauce
    (tinned, packet or home-
    made)
juice of half a lemon
25g/1oz butter
seasoning
chopped parsley

Pre-heat the oven to 190°C/375°F/Gas Mark 5.

1   Fillet the fish (*see* page 10). Season the surface of the fish with salt, pepper and lemon juice. Place prawns on one fillet, cover with second fillet, put into a greased casserole and dot with butter. Cover and cook for 30 minutes.

2   Strain juices into the ready-made white sauce and adjust seasoning as required.

3   The two fillets should have adhered together. Remove all skin if possible, or at least skin from the top surface, place on warmed serving dish, pour over the sauce and sprinkle with chopped parsley.

Serving suggestion: Creamed potatoes, broad beans and courgettes.

Trout au Vin Rosé

Serves 4   Preparation time: 15 minutes   Cooking time: 30 minutes

Oven-baked trout with a rich, subtle sauce.

4 portion-sized trout
4 shallots
150ml/¼ pint rosé wine
150ml/¼ pint thick Hollandaise
    sauce (see page 129)
4 tablespoons double cream
salt and pepper
6 triangles white bread
50g/2oz butter
chopped parsley

Pre-heat the oven to 190°C/375°F/Gas Mark 5.

1 Gut and wash trout thoroughly, preferably leaving heads on.

2 Finely chop shallots and sauté in a little of the butter. Place the trout in a well-buttered baking dish, add shallots and wine, cover the dish with kitchen foil and bake in pre-heated oven for 25 minutes.

3 Lay trout on kitchen paper and remove skins quickly. Cover trout with foil and keep warm. Reserve juices around fish.

4 Pour the juices into a saucepan and reduce liquid by boiling until only a tablespoonful is left. Cool and strain liquid.

5 Add reduced juices to 150ml/¼ pint thick Hollandaise sauce. Add the cream and salt and pepper to taste, and heat sauce gently through. Arrange fish on warmed serving platter and pour sauce over.

Serving suggestion: Garnish with bread triangles fried in butter and parsley. Accompany with minted new potatoes, courgettes and a purée of carrots and parsnips.

Smoked Trout Flaky Roulade

Serves 6   Preparation time: 2½ hours   Cooking time: 35 minutes

Highly suitable for a buffet party.

For the roulade:
225g/8oz plain flour
salt
12g/½oz fresh yeast
½ teaspoon sugar
70ml/2½fl oz milk, warmed
2 egg yolks
100g/4oz butter

For the filling:
1 onion, chopped
75g/3oz cooked patna rice
450g/1lb hot-smoked trout flesh
100g/¼lb cooked shrimps, peeled
75g/3oz melted butter

1   Sieve flour and ½ teaspoon salt into a warm bowl. Make a well. Cream the yeast and sugar together, add warmed milk and pour mixture into well of flour. Mix to a batter in the centre. Cover batter with flour from the sides of the well and leave in a warm place for about 15 minutes.

2   Add egg yolks, mix the whole to a dough. Knead for about 8 minutes. Cover bowl with a damp cloth and leave to rise in a warm place until dough has doubled in size (about 1½ hours).

3   Place dough on a floured board and knock back to original size. Roll out dough into a square. Place flakes of butter on the surface, fold into three like an envelope, roll out again and repeat procedure four times.

4   For the filling, fry onion in butter until golden, add the boiled rice, shrimps and smoked fish (broken into small flakes) and season well.

5   Roll out pastry into a long oblong. Cover with fish mixture and sprinkle with melted butter. Roll up like a swiss roll.

Pre-heat oven to 230°C/450°F/Gas Mark 8.

6   Place roll in a large oiled polythene bag and leave to rise in a warm place for 15–20 minutes, then bake until risen and brown (30–35 minutes).

Serving suggestion: Cut into slices. Serve with mange-tout and ratatouille.

Trout with Caviar

Serves 2   Preparation time: 25 minutes   Cooking time: 25 minutes

Russian-style trout – a dish to impress even the most discerning palate.

2 trout (350g/12oz each)
50g/2oz unsalted butter, melted
225ml/8fl oz double cream
Seasoning
1 tablespoon fresh parsley leaves,
  chopped
1 tablespoon fresh tarragon,
  chopped
1 tablespoon fresh chives,
  chopped
1 tablespoon black lumpfish
  caviar
Fresh lemon juice to taste

---

1 Clean the trout, leaving the head and tail intact. Arrange in a shallow buttered flameproof baking dish. Brush them with a little butter and season.

---

2 Grill the trout under a pre-heated grill about 10cm/4in from the heat, basting them with the remaining butter, for 3–4 minutes each side, or until they start to flake when tested with a fork.

---

3 Transfer the trout to a heated serving plate. Cover and keep warm.

---

4 Add the cream to the baking dish and, over a moderate heat, mix with the remaining trout scraps. Strain this mixture into a saucepan. Reduce the mixture over a moderately high heat until it thickens slightly. Stir in the parsley, tarragon and chives. Simmer the sauce for 1 minute. Remove the pan from the heat, stir in the caviar, lemon juice and season once more to taste.

Serving suggestion: Spoon the sauce over the trout to serve.

Trout with Spinach

Serves 4   Preparation time: 20 minutes   Cooking time: 15 minutes

A colourful and attractive party dish using filleted trout.

2 large trout (900g/2lb each)
1 tablespoon vinegar
1 onion, peeled and sliced
1 onion, peeled and chopped
*   finely*
1 tablespoon light cooking oil
water
salt and ground black pepper
50g/2oz butter
1 tablespoon lemon juice
pinch of nutmeg
1/4 teaspoon dried mixed herbs
275ml/1/2 pint white sauce
*   (packet, tinned or home-*
*   made)*
1 tablespoon medium sherry
1 packet frozen chopped spinach
tomato slices and chopped
*   parsley for garnish*

---

1 Fillet the trout into 4 portions (*see* page 10). Place water, sliced onion, vinegar and salt in a pan and bring to simmering point. Immerse fillets, simmer for 5 minutes and turn off heat, keeping fish warm in the liquid.

---

2 Heat oil in a pan, add chopped onion and cook until tender. Add 2 tablespoons of the poaching liquid, lemon juice and spinach. Cook gently until just tender. Drain surplus liquid, and mix in butter, nutmeg and herbs.

---

3 Prepare white sauce and add sherry.

---

4 Place spinach in a layer on a warm serving plate. Lay the fish down the centre and spoon the sauce over it. Top with slices of tomato and sprinkle with parsley.

Serving suggestion: Creamed potato, braised celery, sweetcorn.

100

Indonesian Stuffed Trout

Serves 4   Preparation time: 20 minutes   Cooking time: 25 minutes

Steam-cooked trout with a fruity, spicy filling.

4 portion-sized trout
1 medium onion, chopped
1 clove of garlic, crushed
1 small root ginger, crushed
1 cup fresh white breadcrumbs
1 small tin crushed pineapple
1 teaspoon coriander powder
salt and pepper
1 egg, beaten
4 large blanched cabbage leaves
light oil for frying

1 Wash and gut trout, and fillet out bones, leaving heads and tails intact (*see* page 10).

2 Toss the onion, garlic and ginger in hot oil until softened. In the same pan mix in the breadcrumbs, pineapple, coriander powder, salt and pepper. Turn off the heat and then bind mixture with the egg.

3 Divide filling into four and pack into fish cavities. Wrap each fish securely in a blanched cabbage leaf, and place in a steamer to cook for about 20 minutes.

4 Remove cabbage leaves and put fish into very hot frying oil for a few minutes on each side to brown skins.

Serving suggestion: Serve with a savoury rice into which you have mixed peas and corn with peppers.

Trout in Wine and Vegetable Sauce

Serves 4   Preparation time: 20 minutes   Cooking time: 30 minutes

This is a dish of baked trout in a simple sauce which is cooked around the fish and then puréed.

4 portion-sized trout
salt and pepper
parsley
basil
chopped chives
garlic
50g/2oz butter
roughly chopped fresh
    vegetables, as available, for
    example, leeks, mushrooms,
    onions, carrots, shallots,
    celery
175ml/6fl oz medium white wine

Pre-heat the oven to 190°C/375°F/Gas Mark 5.

1 Clean and gut fish, retaining or removing heads as required.

2 Combine the herbs and seasoning with the butter and pack mixture into cavities. Place the fish in a lidded casserole dish and surround with a mixture of chopped fresh vegetables. Cover with wine. Place in pre-heated oven and bake for 25 minutes.

3 Set fish aside and keep warm.

4 Put the juices and vegetables into a blender and purée until smooth. Pour the sauce over the fish.

Serving suggestion: Duchesse potatoes and broad beans.

CHAPTER 4

BARBECUE DISHES

Barbecue Trout with Sweetcorn

Serves 4   Preparation time: 15 minutes   Cooking time: 15 minutes

For this recipe you will need fresh corn on the cob still in their husks. Your guests will be surprised and delighted by the novel presentation of this dish.

4 small trout
salt and freshly ground black
 pepper
4 rashers rindless sweetcure
 bacon
4 large corn on the cob in the
 husk
75g/3oz butter

1 Gut and clean the trout, removing heads and tails. Season inside and out. Loosely roll each rasher of bacon and place inside cavity.

2 Remove the corn from the husks, being careful to keep leaves undamaged. Put each trout into an empty husk and tie up the end to encase fish.

3 Clean the fibres from the corn and boil cobs in water for 10–15 minutes until tender.

4 While the corn is boiling cook the trout in the husks over the barbecue, turning occasionally, for about 15 minutes.

To serve: Remove trout from husks and put on individual plates with cobs of corn rolled in butter and seasoned with salt and pepper.

Barbecue Baked Trout

Serves 6   Preparation time: 10 minutes   Cooking time: 12 minutes

Trout cooked in foil and served with a deliciously spicy barbecue sauce.

6 rainbow or brown trout
75g/3oz butter
6 sprigs fresh thyme
3 lemons
salt and pepper

For the sauce (makes about
    425ml/15fl oz):
425ml/15fl oz cider vinegar
150ml/¼ pint water
3 tablespoons sugar
2 tablespoons made English
    mustard
2 cloves garlic, crushed
salt and pepper
4 tablespoons tomato purée
grated zest and juice of 1 lemon
50g/2oz butter

---

1 To make the sauce, mix all the ingredients together and simmer for 20 minutes. Serve hot.

---

2 Gut, clean and de-head trout. Pat dry. Liberally butter sides and cavity of fish and put a sprig of thyme in each, with a little grated zest of lemon.

---

3 Wrap securely in foil parcels, pouring in a little lemon juice before sealing. (Remember that if the foil is used 'dull' side out there is less risk of burning.)

---

4 Cook the parcels over the barbecue for about 6 minutes on each side.

Serving suggestion: Mashed potato, buttered steamed white cabbage and barbecue sauce.

Wine-Baked Barbecue Trout

Serves 4   Preparation time: 10 minutes   Cooking time: 12 minutes

Barbecued trout with a more sophisticated flavour.

4 whole trout (275g/10oz each)
4 wedges lemon
8 large crisp lettuce leaves
50g/2oz butter
1 large sliced onion
4 tablespoons chopped parsley
225ml/8fl oz dry white wine
salt and pepper

---

1   Clean and gut trout, removing head. Immerse in boiling water for 30 seconds to assist removal of skin. Pat dry with kitchen paper.

---

2   Sprinkle salt and pepper inside and out. Place a piece of lemon inside each cavity.

---

3   Cut four sheets of kitchen foil large enough to wrap each trout. Place a lettuce leaf on each piece, then a dot of butter. Put the fish on top, then slices of onion and another dot of butter, a tablespoon of chopped parsley and finally another lettuce leaf.

---

4   Before completely sealing the parcel, pour a quarter of the wine into each one. When wrapped securely, bake on grill rack over fire for 5–6 minutes each side.

Serving suggestion: Have hot jacket potatoes ready which have been well cooked and had a cross cut on top. Squeeze these to fluff up the potato inside, and pour the juices from the foil parcels into the potatoes. Serve the fish on individual plates, with a generous helping of fried mushrooms as a pleasant accompaniment.

Marinated Barbecue Trout

Serves 4   Preparation time: 15 minutes (plus marinating time: 1 hour)   Cooking time: 10 minutes

Extra flavoursome trout baked over the barbecue with a marinade which mades a good sauce.

4 portion-sized trout
4 tablespoons soy sauce
2 tablespoons lemon juice
2 tablespoons olive oil
25g/1oz fresh dill, chives or
  sorrel, chopped
1 tablespoon caster sugar
4 knobs of butter
cornflour to thicken sauce

1 Clean and gut the trout, removing heads. Lie them in a shallow dish.

2 Mix together all the ingredients except the butter and the cornflour. Pour this marinade over the trout and leave for at least 1 hour.

3 Cut four large pieces of foil and place a knob of butter on each. Lie trout on top and wrap securely in foil. Cook over the barbecue for about 5 minutes on each side.

4 Bring marinade to the boil in a pan and thicken juices with a little cornflour to make a sauce.

Serving suggestion: Open foil parcels carefully, add juices to the sauce and stir in. Put each trout on a plate and spoon sauce over. Serve with boiled potatoes garnished with parsley and butter, and tinned celery hearts which have been warmed through.

Smokey Baked Potatoes

Serves 6   Preparation time: 10 minutes   Cooking time: 1 hour 20 minutes

A jacket potato dish with a difference. Try this at your next Bonfire Night party.

6 large potatoes
450g/1lb hot-smoked trout
150ml/¼ pint milk
12g/½oz butter
12g/½oz flour
salt and pepper
1 egg yolk

1 Scrub potatoes and bake at 220°C/425°F/Gas Mark 7 for approximately 1 hour.

2 Separate the head, skin and bones from the flesh of the fish. Simmer all but the flesh in milk for 6 minutes. Strain the milk and retain.

3 Melt butter in a pan, add flour and stir to a paste. Gradually pour in sufficient milk to make a thick sauce. Season with salt and pepper and stir and simmer for 5 minutes to cook sauce. Flake fish and add to the sauce.

4 When the potatoes are soft, cut them in half and remove the potato from the jackets. Place potato in a bowl with egg yolk and sauce. Beat until mixture is creamy.

5 Pile mixture back into jackets and brown under a hot grill before serving.

Serving suggestion: Serve these with tomatoes baked while the oven is on for the potatoes and a bitter-sharp salad of watercress, endives and onion rings.

Barbecued Trout

A trout barbecue makes an original alternative to steak, sausages and chicken. No method of cooking could be simpler and the charcoal-cooked flavour of both the flesh and the crispy skin is almost unbeatable.

a batch of portion-sized trout
flour
salt
pepper

charcoal
a handful of hardwood shavings

1 Prepare the fire well in advance so that the charcoal is red and glowing.

2 Gut fish, leaving heads on. Scrub the skins well and pat dry in kitchen paper or newspaper. Toss the fish in flour which has been seasoned with salt and pepper.

3 Charcoal grill on both sides until the flesh is ready to part from the bone. To serve, remove heads and tails.

Serving suggestion: Accompany with a baked jacket potato and either a salad or cold ratatouille. Canned barbecue sauces are now readily available if required.

CHAPTER 5

COLD DISHES

Smoked Trout Salad

Serves 4   Preparation time: 15 minutes

Two attractive ways of presenting a smoked trout salad – easy to serve and bone-free.

1 hot-smoked trout (275g/10oz)
½ small cucumber
6 radishes
4 stalks of celery
2 spring onions
175ml/6fl oz mayonnaise
crisp lettuce leaves
salt and pepper

1 Remove the trout flesh from the bone and rough-flake. Dice unpeeled cucumber, slice radishes into thin rings, and chop spring onions finely.

2 Mix the fish, vegetables, mayonnaise and seasoning together. Place crisp lettuce leaves around the edge of a large serving plate and pile the mixture in the centre.

For an alternative salad:
sultanas soaked in lemon juice
chopped walnuts
chopped apples
salad cream
smoked, flaked trout

1 Mix together and pile on to crisp lettuce as above.

2 Serve with warm granary bread.

Cold-Smoked Trout Quiche

Serves 4   Preparation time: 40 minutes   Cooking time: 40 minutes

This luxury quiche can be made with smoked salmon off-cuts, but hopefully you will be able to dip into your store of frozen cold-smoked trout.

225g/8oz shortcrust pastry
175g/6oz cold-smoked trout
2 tablespoons chopped fresh
    chives or parsley
freshly ground black pepper
salt
3 eggs
125ml/4fl oz double cream
125ml/4fl oz milk

Pre-heat the oven to 230°C/450°F/Gas Mark 8.

1   Roll out pastry and line a 20cm/8in flan case. Chill for 30 minutes then blind bake until lightly cooked. Allow to cool.

2   Finely slice the fish and lay in flan case. Sprinkle with chives or parsley, and season with black pepper and salt (unless the fish itself is somewhat salty). Beat the liquid ingredients together and pour into case.

3   Place flan in oven and reduce heat to 190°C/375°F/Gas Mark 5 for approximately 30 minutes or until flan has set. Serve hot or cold. If only lightly set this quiche will reheat beautifully.

Trout and Rice Savoury Salad

Serves 4–6   Preparation time: 20 minutes

This dish is very suitable for a summer buffet table.

175g/6oz ready-cooked trout flesh
225g/8oz cooked patna rice
2 tablespoons thick mayonnaise
small tin of sweetcorn with
    peppers
¼ teaspoon white pepper
½ teaspoon onion salt
few drops tabasco sauce
tomato slices for garnish

1 Flake the trout.

2 Mix all the ingredients together, pack into an oiled glass mould or bowl, and
   press firmly down.

3 Refrigerate until thoroughly chilled.

Serving suggestion: Turn out mould on to a large serving platter, surround
with shredded lettuce and garnish with tomato slices. Serve with a range of other
buffet dishes.

Cold Poached Trout

Preparation time: 5 minutes   Cooking time: 5 minutes

This is a traditional method of serving cold trout, particularly the larger fish from 900g/2lb upwards. Note that the same cooking time applies regardless of the size of the fish.

a 1.4kg/3lb trout will serve 4–6
water to cover fish
salt
vinegar

1 Gut and wash the fish, preferably leaving the head on. Fill a fish kettle or suitably long deep baking dish with water, season with plenty of salt, and add 2–3 tablespoons of vinegar.
   Note Adding wine, vegetables, bouquet garni and so on to the poaching liquid will marginally alter the flavour, and is a matter of personal preference and experimentation.

2 Immerse the fish in the cold water, which should barely cover the skin. Bring water to the boil, and simmer gently for 5 minutes. Turn off the heat and allow fish to cool in the liquid.

3 Remove fish from the liquid, and skin carefully, preserving the head and tail intact for attractive presentation. Glaze with aspic (optional) or cover with clear film and refrigerate.

Serving suggestion: Garnish attractively before serving with a selection of salads. Try serving with an avocado and watercress mayonnaise (*see* page 123).

Smoked Trout Mousse

Serves 6   Preparation time: 25 minutes

This dish is a gourmet's delight, either as a main course for a special luncheon, or serving 6–8 as an entrée. Preparation time presumes you have some smoked trout to hand, otherwise add smoking time for fresh trout.

225g/8oz cooked smoked trout
40g/1½oz gelatine
2–3 tablespoons hot water
400ml/14fl oz tin of lobster, crab
* or scampi cream soup*
150ml/¼ pint double cream,
* whipped*
150ml/¼ pint salad cream
few prawns for decoration
watercress for garnish
lemon slices for garnish

1 Dissolve gelatine in water and mix into tinned soup.

2 Flake fish finely, removing any skin or bones, and fold the fish, whipped cream and salad cream into the soup.

3 Oil a suitable mould or tin. Place a few prawns decoratively in the base, pour in the mixture and refrigerate until set.

Serving suggestion: Turn out on to a serving dish and garnish with watercress sprigs and lemon slices. Serve with hot bread rolls and various salads.

Terrine of Smoked and Fresh Trout

Serves 6–8   Preparation time: 25 minutes   Cooking time: 10 minutes

This dish may be made a few days in advance as it will keep well in the refrigerator. Individual slices make an ideal entrée.

800g/1¾lb trout
100g/4oz finely sliced cold-
    smoked trout (or smoked
    salmon)
1½ sachets of gelatine
575ml/1 pint milk
few drops of cochineal
150ml/¼ pint whipped cream
knob of butter
salt and paprika
cucumber slices and lemon
    wedges for garnish

1 Wash, gut and remove head of trout. Poach for 10 minutes in milk seasoned with salt and paprika.

2 Remove fish from liquid, remove skin and bones and flake flesh. Strain milk and return to pan.

3 Dissolve gelatine in milk, allow to cool until about to set, and then mix in a couple of drops of cochineal and the whipped cream.

4 Line a buttered terrine with slices of smoked trout. Mix the flaked poached trout with the sauce and fill terrine. Cover the top with slices of smoked trout. Cover and refrigerate until set.

Serving suggestion: Turn terrine out on to serving dish and decorate with cucumber and lemon slices. Serve individual portions sliced through the terrine as an entrée, and accompany with brown bread and butter.

CHAPTER 6

IDEAS FOR SANDWICHES, DIPS AND SPREADS

SANDWICHES

- Cold-smoked salmon trout in fine slices between brown bread and butter, seasoned with lemon juice and cayenne pepper.
- Flaked hot-smoked trout with cucumber or finely sliced celery pieces.
- Flaked hot-smoked trout pieces with chopped cooked bacon.

SANDWICH SPREAD

- 2 parts smoked fish, finely flaked, to one part crushed pineapple pieces, well drained. Bind with mayonnaise to spreading consistency, season with black pepper and salt.
- 2 parts smoked fish to one part chopped gherkins, bound with salad cream to spreading consistency.

Trout Cocktail Dip

Serves 8 or makes numerous canapés

Trout pieces dipped in a beer batter and deep-fried, served with a cocktail sauce. Also suitable as an entrée.

4 filleted pieces of trout
light vegetable oil for deep frying

For the batter:
1 cup plain flour
1 egg
¾ cup beer
¼ cup water
salt and pepper

For the sauce:
1 small carton thick natural
*   yoghurt*
1 tablespoon lemon juice
squeeze of tomato purée (from a
*   tube)*
1 tablespoon brandy
2 teaspoons Worcester sauce
drop of tabasco
salt

1 To make the sauce, mix all the ingredients together until they are creamy.

2 Cut the raw trout into small pieces.

3 Make the batter. Put the flour and seasoning in a bowl, beat in the egg, and add the liquids slowly, beating all the time. Allow batter to rest for 30 minutes and beat again before using.

4 Dip the trout into the batter and deep-fry in oil. They will only take a few seconds each and are best done one at a time to prevent sticking.

Serving suggestion: Put a small bowl of sauce on a large plate, surround with fish and provide cocktail sticks for dipping.

Smoked Trout and Cheese Dip

1½ cups smoked flaked fish
175g/6oz cream cheese
1 clove garlic, finely minced (or
   garlic salt)
3 tablespoons minced onion
¼ teaspoon salt (unless garlic
   salt is used)
1 tablespoon lemon juice
1 tablespoon finely chopped red/
   green peppers
150ml/¼ pint whipped cream or
   plain yoghurt

1 Mash all the ingredients except cream together or place in food processor for
   a few seconds.

2 Blend in cream or yoghurt. Serve with crisps or slices of fresh raw vegetables
   such as carrot, celery and cauliflower sprigs.

Smoked Trout Paste

A delightful smooth spreading paste can be made by blending the trout flesh
with a small quantity of strongly-seasoned roux – milk (flavoured by boiling
with bones), and a little melted butter. Pack in small jars and freeze until
required.

Quick Trout Spread

¼ teaspoon curry powder
1 small clove garlic, crushed
1 tablespoon capers, chopped
1 tablespoon chopped parsley
¼ teaspoon oregano
3 tablespoons sour cream
flaked flesh from one poached
*   trout*

Mix all the ingredients together in a blender. Serve with bread or rolls which
have been warmed through.

CHAPTER 7

SAUCES

A sauce is used to flavour, coat or accompany a dish, and it may also be used in the actual cooking in order to bind ingredients together. It has to be carefully chosen as it can enhance the flavour of trout in perfect condition, or mask what might be a fish in poor condition. It is hoped that most anglers will recognise an out-of-condition fish that will inevitably turn black, and will return it to the water to grow on for next season – even the cat will turn its nose up at such a dish!

We have all known and suffered from a tasteless, badly-made white sauce, but a carefully-made plain sauce, which is the basis of so many others, has great culinary value. Various ingredients can be added to this basic sauce – extra butter, mushrooms, asparagus tips, lemon juice, cream, cheese, egg yolk, tomato purée – according to what the fish recipe may suggest, or it may be a simple accompaniment to one of the vegetables. Two sauces with a meal are not recommended as they will rival each other and divert the eater's attention from the main ingredient.

There are two basic methods for white sauce:

Roux Method

20g/³⁄₄oz butter or margarine
20g/³⁄₄oz flour
275ml/½ pint milk (or milk and
*   stock)*
salt and pepper

1   Melt the fat in the pan and stir in the flour. Stir over a gentle heat for a few minutes; do not let flour brown.

2   Remove pan from the heat and pour in the liquid gradually, stirring well to prevent lumps forming.

3   Return to the heat and boil for 5 minutes to cook the flour. Season to taste.

Blended Method

15–20g/$^{1}/_{2}$–$^{3}/_{4}$oz flour (or $^{1}/_{4}$–$^{1}/_{2}$oz
cornflour)
275ml/$^{1}/_{2}$ pint milk or milk and
stock (from vegetables or fish
juices)
knob of butter
salt and pepper

1   Blend the flour with a little of the liquid and bring the rest of the liquid to the boil. Pour the liquid on to the blended flour, stirring well.

2   Cook for 5 minutes, continuing to stir, then beat in the butter and season to taste.

Both these methods will give you a sauce of pouring consistency. Use an extra 7g/$^{1}/_{4}$oz flour if you need a coating consistency. If you want to make a richer sauce, add butter, cream or egg yolk, but reheat (don't re-boil) after these additions, otherwise the sauce may curdle.

Variations on the Basic White Sauce

Anchovy or Shrimp

Make 275ml/$^{1}/_{2}$ pint sauce with milk and fish stock. Add a teaspoon of anchovy or shrimp essence. Alternatively, pound in a mortar equal weights of shrimps and unsalted butter (or use potted shrimps), and colour with a few drops of cochineal, or tomato purée. Blend in with the sauce.

Caper Sauce

Make 275ml/$^{1}/_{2}$ pint basic sauce with milk and fish stock. Add a tablespoonful of chopped capers and a tablespoon of caper vinegar.

Cheese Sauce

Add 2 tablespoonfuls of strong grated cheese and $^{1}/_{2}$ teaspoonful made mustard to basic sauce.

Egg Sauce

Add one or two finely chopped hard-boiled eggs to 275ml/½ pint sauce.

Fennel Sauce

Cook 225g/8oz fennel until tender, chop very finely and add to sauce.

Onion Sauce

Sauté about 3 tablespoonfuls of chopped onion in the fat before adding the flour, or purée 2 medium boiled onions, make the sauce with ½ milk/½ water (using the water in which onions were cooked), and blend purée with sauce.

Parsley Sauce

Add 1 tablespoonful of finely chopped fresh parsley to 275ml/½ pint sauce or simmer 100g/4oz parsley heads until tender, add to sauce and purée in blender.

Brown Sauce (Roux Method)

1 small onion
1 small carrot
1 piece turnip
20g/³⁄₄oz dripping
20g/³⁄₄oz flour
150ml/¹⁄₄ pint stock
salt and pepper

Peel and slice the vegetables. Fry onion in the dripping, stir in flour and cook it until golden-brown. Remove from heat. Stir in stock gradually, add other vegetables, simmer for 25–30 minutes, season and purée in blender.

Variations on Brown Sauce

Piquante Sauce

Replace half the stock with sherry or white wine and include a bouquet garni. Simmer 2 shallots and a small bunch of thyme in 150ml/¹⁄₄ pint vinegar, add to the sauce at blender stage and finally add two finely chopped gherkins.

Spanish Sauce

To the basic brown sauce add one dessertspoon of mushroom ketchup and one dessertspoon of tomato purée.

Tuna Sauce

200g/7oz can tuna in oil
275ml/½ pint mayonnaise
juice of 1 lemon
50g/2oz can anchovy fillets
6 tablespoons chicken stock or
    fish stock
salt and black pepper

Place all ingredients, including oil from tuna, into a blender and blend until smooth. Either dress cold poached trout with the sauce and garnish, or heat without bringing to the boil and serve with hot poached trout.

Béchamel Sauce

575ml/1 pint milk
1 shallot
1 small carrot
1 stick celery
1 bay leaf
6 peppercorns
50g/2oz butter
50g/2oz flour
salt and pepper

Put all the vegetables and flavourings into the milk and simmer for 20 minutes. Strain the liquid. Fry the flour in the fat, gradually add the stock, stirring continuously to prevent lumps forming, and cook for 7 minutes. Add seasoning to taste and up to 150ml/¼ pint double cream to 1 pint sauce for added richness if required. (Reheat but do not boil after cream has been added.)

Avocado and Watercress Mayonnaise

175ml/6oz mayonnaise
2 large avocados
2 bunches of watercress
juice of 1 lemon
salt and pepper
pinch of bicarbonate of soda

De-stone and skin avocado, chop and toss in lemon juice. De-stem watercress and poach for 5 minutes in salted water with pinch of bicarbonate of soda to retain colour. Strain, season and purée all ingredients. Chill and serve with cold poached trout or trout terrine.

White Wine Sauce

575ml/1 pint basic white sauce
*   made with strongly fish-*
*   flavoured stock and milk*
275ml/½ pint additional fish
*   stock*
75ml/3fl oz dry white wine
2 egg yolks
2 tablespoons thick double cream
1 tablespoon mushroom ketchup
50g/2oz unsalted butter

Add the wine to the fish stock and simmer until reduced to one tablespoonful. Mix with white sauce and mushroom ketchup, and stir continuously until boiling point is reached. Strain this sauce, beat together egg yolks and cream and whisk into sauce; add butter in flakes. Keep warm over hot water in double saucepan.

Hot Mayonnaise Sauce

50g/2oz flour
1 level teaspoon mustard powder
1 level teaspoon salt
25g/1oz sugar
2 small egg yolks
350ml/12fl oz hot milk
50ml/2fl oz wine vinegar
50g/2oz butter
125ml/4fl oz double cream

Into a blender put flour, salt, mustard, sugar and egg yolks. Blend for a few seconds, turn to slow speed and continue to blend while pouring in hot milk. Put into bowl set over pan of hot water. Continue to beat with hand whisk until the consistency of real mayonnaise is reached, slip in wine vinegar and butter in small knobs. Finally, when ready to serve, blend in the double cream. A circle of wet greaseproof paper on top will prevent a skin forming if the sauce is not required immediately.

Hungarian Sauce

50g/2oz minced onion
25g/1oz vegetable oil
25g/1oz flour
275ml/½ pint chopped tinned
*   tomatoes*
150ml/¼ pint cream
1 teaspoon paprika

Brown the onion in the oil, shake in the flour and cook for 2 minutes. Slowly add pulped tomatoes. Simmer for 5 minutes. Add paprika and cream just before serving. (Do not boil once cream has been added.)

Tomato Sauce

175g/6oz tomatoes
1 small onion
1 clove garlic
150ml/¼ pint milk
1 teaspoon ground mace
1 teaspoon ginger
1 teaspoon paprika
salt and pepper
1 teaspoon sugar
25g/1oz soft butter
2 teaspoons flour

Finely chop onion and mince garlic, and fry very slowly together without browning until tender. Add the skinned and pulped tomatoes (or tinned tomatoes), and simmer for 5 minutes. Rub the flour into the soft butter to make 'pellets', and add these one at a time, stirring continually. Add spices, sugar and seasoning. Stir milk in drips, simmer for 5 minutes. Serve hot.

A piquant variation: Add 25g/1oz chopped gherkin, 25g/1oz chopped capers and/or 25g/1oz chopped sultanas which have previously been soaked for 1 hour in the juice of half a lemon.

Chive Sauce

100g/4oz unsalted butter
25g/1oz chopped chives
25g/1oz chopped shallots
4 tablespoons dry white wine
2 tablespoons double cream

Put 25g/1oz butter in a small saucepan over moderate heat, add the shallots and cook slowly until tender without browning. Add the white wine and then the cream, bring to the boil and reduce by half. When reduced, turn down the heat and whisk in the remaining diced butter piece by piece until incorporated with the sauce. Season with salt and pepper. Add chopped chives. Serve hot.

Gooseberry Sauce

Traditionally served with mackerel, but delightful with poached or grilled trout.

Make 275ml/½ pint white sauce. Add 225g/½lb stewed and puréed gooseberries, a little ground ginger or grated nutmeg, 1 teaspoon sugar, and a squeeze of lemon juice.

Horseradish Cream

Mix 2 tablespoons of grated fresh horseradish with 2 tablespoons double cream. Add 2 teaspoons of lemon juice, a pinch of salt and a pinch of sugar. No cooking is required.

Tuna and Mushroom Sauce

175g/6oz mushrooms, chopped
½ clove garlic, crushed
25g/1oz butter
200g/7oz tin tuna (in brine)
150ml/¼ pint double cream
425ml/¾ pint béchamel sauce
    (see page 122)
salt and black pepper

Fry the mushrooms and garlic gently in butter. When-softened add flaked tuna and cream, place in liquidiser and purée. The purée is now ready to be incorporated with the béchamel sauce, seasoned with salt and black pepper as necessary. Gently reheat.

The combination of tuna and mushroom is an unusual one, but it makes a particularly delicious sauce.

Herb Sauce

425ml/³⁄₄ pint béchamel sauce
150ml/¹⁄₄ pint double cream
small handful spinach leaves
chives
tarragon
parsley
watercress
1 glass dry white wine

Chop all the green ingredients and simmer gently in the wine. When softened and tender, add the cream and liquidise. Add purée gradually to béchamel sauce, tasting as you add, as the purée is a very strong seasoning and you may not need it all.

Herb and Lemon Sauce

(Makes 300ml/10fl oz)

15g/¹⁄₂oz butter
1 crushed clove garlic
15ml/1 tablespoon flour
300ml/10fl oz milk
¹⁄₂ teaspoon dried thyme
1 tablespoon chopped chives
grated rind 1 lemon
1 teaspoon lemon juice
1 tablespoon double cream
salt and black pepper

Melt the butter in a saucepan and fry garlic for 4–5 minutes. Off the heat stir in the flour and make a paste. Gradually add milk, stirring constantly. Stir in herbs and seasoning. Return pan to heat and simmer for 15 minutes, stirring from time to time. Remove from heat. Stir in lemon juice and cream. Serve hot in a sauce-boat. Delicious with hot poached trout.

Cider Sauce

1 medium onion, chopped
150g/5oz butter
1 pint cider
bones and trimmings from fish
bouquet garni
3 tablespoons flour
2 egg yolks
50ml/2fl oz double cream
juice of ½ lemon
salt and pepper

Fry onion until soft in 25g/1oz butter. Pour in cider plus 150ml/¼ pint water, add fish bones, bouquet garni and seasoning. Simmer steadily for half an hour with lid off – stock should reduce by a quarter. Make a roux with 50g/2oz butter and flour, add strained stock and boil for 7 minutes. Take off heat and gradually beat in the egg yolks and cream. Do not boil when reheating. Add last 50g/2oz butter, lemon juice and seasoning just before serving.

Simple Butter Sauce

juices from the pan
100g/4oz butter
150ml/¼ pint double cream
lemon juice
chives or parsley, chopped
salt and pepper

Into the juices in the frying pan melt the butter; pour in the cream, mix and simmer for about 5 minutes, season, add lemon juice and finally the chives or parsley. As a variation, substitute the chives or parsley with 1 tablespoon chopped mixed herbs and a tablespoon of chopped capers and/or a dessertspoon of tomato purée.

Hollandaise Sauce

This is a delicate classical sauce, not unlike a hot mayonnaise. It is traditionally served with fish, and also as an accompaniment to vegetables such as asparagus and globe artichokes.

2 tablespoons fish stock or water
1 dessertspoon tarragon vinegar
2 egg yolks
50g/2oz butter
1 dessertspoon lemon juice
salt and cayenne pepper

Put the stock or water, vinegar and egg yolks into a basin and stand this in a saucepan of hot water. Whisk over heat until the sauce thickens. Remove from heat and add the butter in small knobs one by one, stirring well. Add lemon juice and season to taste. The sauce must not boil.

Mock Hollandaise

To 275ml/½ pint basic roux white sauce in a double saucepan, add 2 beaten egg yolks and 2 tablespoons cream. Do not allow to boil. Add a little lemon juice or white wine vinegar before serving to give a sharper taste.

Variations: Add grated rind of blood orange and juice; add 3–4 teaspoons caviare; or substitute lemon juice with medium-sweet sherry.

Sauce Aioli

1 clove garlic
200g/7oz boiled potato
1 egg yolk
1 tablespoon lemon juice
5 tablespoons olive oil
salt and pepper

Place all ingredients (except olive oil) in a blender and purée until smooth. Gradually add oil while blender is running until a rich sauce is produced.

Tartare Sauce

A sharp, piquant sauce, traditional with many fish dishes. A simple version can be made by finely chopping capers and cocktail gherkins and combining with bought or home-made salad cream. For a more sophisticated version, you will need the following.

2 eggs (hard-boiled)
1 raw egg yolk
275ml/½ pint olive or light
 vegetable oil
1 tablespoon malt vinegar
1 teaspoon chopped parsley
1 teaspoon chopped chives
1 teaspoon chopped capers
1 teaspoon chopped cocktail
 gherkins

Slice hard-boiled eggs in half, remove yolks, mash together with raw egg yolk, blend well together and season. In a blender place egg yolk mixture and add oil drop by drop as in making a mayonnaise. Dilute with vinegar, and finally mix in the chopped herbs by hand. For additional bulk and texture add, if required, the chopped white of one of the hard-boiled eggs.

Court Bouillon

'Court bouillon' is the term used for a liquid suitable for poaching fish. Ideally a fish kettle should be used, but an alternative receptacle would be a wide grill pan with a 'lid' of aluminium foil.

3.3 litres/6 pints cold water
2 tablespoons salt
150ml/¼ pint vinegar
1 onion, sliced
1 carrot, sliced
1 teaspoon pepper
1 bouquet garni

Bring all the ingredients to the boil, reduce heat and simmer for 1 hour. Strain and use liquid as required. A quantity can be frozen into blocks for future use.

Fish Stock

This recipe is for a tastier version of court bouillon. You may have sufficient juices in the pan or casserole not to need additional stock. However, if you are cooking a variety of fish dishes, soups and sauces, it would be wise to make up a good quantity of tasty fish stock and freeze it in blocks for future use. A fishmonger may give you bones or at least charge very little for them – turbot and sole bones have a high gelatine content and are particularly good. The bones from your smoked trout are invaluable as are the backbones from filleting out large trout prior to smoking (reserve any useful bones in a bag in the freezer).

700–1150g/2–3lb fish trimmings
1 large onion, sliced
1 medium carrot, sliced
1 small stick celery
10 peppercorns
1 dessertspoon white wine
*   vinegar*
150ml/¼ pint dry white wine (or
*   double the amount of vinegar*
*   and add 2 teaspoons sugar)*
water

Place all the ingredients into a large covered pan with enough water to cover adequately (do not include salt at this stage, as it may lead to oversalting the final product). Simmer for ½ hour, then strain.

Aspic Jelly

This can be made by adding gelatine to your fish stock; how much can best be judged when the stock is cold and natural gelatine content is evident. You will need to season the jelly and possibly clarify it (in other words, make it a clear jelly).

To clarify: Use 1 eggshell and 1 egg white per 575ml/1 pint of liquid jelly. Crush the eggshell, mix with the egg white, and add to the liquid. The pan should not be more than half-full as it may easily boil over. Bring to boiling point, whisking all the time. Stop whisking, allow the froth to rise. Take the pan from the heat and allow to stand for 5 minutes. Strain jelly through muslin.

CHAPTER 8

VEGETABLE
ACCOMPANIMENTS

There are certain vegetables which are unpopular with fish, possibly because of their strong flavours. Cabbage, marrow, sprouts, swede, pumpkin, parsnip, carrots and cauliflower are some of these, yet they need not all be ruled out, as an unconventional way of serving them can turn out to be surprisingly good. In alphabetical order I give a list of appropriate vegetables that are readily available and suggest some ways of preparing them.

Artichokes (Jerusalem) To fry: scrub well, neaten with potato peeler if necessary, slice thinly and fry in very hot fat. Drain, serve hot.
To boil: scrub well, peel thinly. Divide into roughly 5cm/2in pieces and boil for 10–15 minutes in lightly salted water until tender. Drain and serve hot with a pat of butter or in a white sauce.

Artichokes (Globe) Either hot or cold the tinned variety of artichoke hearts are delicious, although an acquired taste.

Asparagus Trim white ends, tie in a loose bundle and boil for some 20 minutes until all the green is tender. Tinned or frozen asparagus are easier and nearly as delicious.

Aubergine To fry: peel and slice 7mm/⅓in thick, sprinkle with salt and pepper, then flour. Fry a few slices of onion in a little fat until they change colour, then add the slices of aubergine and cook like pancakes.
To bake: do not peel. Cut in half lengthwise, and arrange flesh side up in a casserole dish. Run the point of a knife round the inside of the skin and score across the flesh. Dot with butter and bake in a medium oven for 30 minutes.

Beet To boil: wash carefully, avoiding scraping or cutting, boil in salted water for 1–2 hours, according to size, or more quickly in a pressure cooker. To serve hot, peel when done, slice thinly and sprinkle lemon juice over.

Broad Beans Boil until tender, serve with butter and chopped parsley, or in a parsley or light cheese sauce.

Broccoli Plunge into boiling water for 10–12 minutes. Drain, serve with melted butter or a light sauce, or after draining brown lightly in butter and serve hot with grated cheese sprinkled over.

Carrots Scrape and cut into small pieces. Boil 15–20 minutes until tender, drain and stir in a knob of butter and a teaspoonful of bottled mint sauce.

Cauliflower Parboil florets, dip in batter and deep fry.

Celeriac Peel, cut into small chunks and boil gently for 10–15 minutes until tender. Serve buttered or in a light sauce.

Celery To braise: in a casserole dish with butter, salt and a little brown sugar, cover and cook in a low oven for 2 hours or until tender. Tinned celery hearts are a simple and popular accompaniment gently heated through and covered with finely chopped hard-boiled egg.

Chestnuts Slit and roast until done (if tinned, warm through), peel while hot and toss in butter.

Chicory Place 450g/1lb of washed and trimmed chicory in a casserole, with 25g/1oz butter, juice of half a lemon, ¼ cup of water and seasoning. Braise for 1 hour.

Corn on the Cob Tinned or frozen, serve with hot melted butter.

Courgettes (Zucchini) The courgette is a very versatile vegetable. It can be boiled whole until tender, then diced, or thinly sliced and fried in bacon fat or butter on its own, or with onions. The following is one of the most delicious ways to cook it, which looks very pretty and is easy to make.

Serves 4–6
450g/1lb courgettes
1 teaspoon salt
65g/2½oz butter
freshly ground pepper
pinch of nutmeg

Wash and trim the vegetables, coarse-grate by hand or in a food processor. Place in colander, sprinkle with the salt, toss and leave for 30 minutes. Rinse under cold tap and shake or pat dry. Heat butter in saucepan over medium heat, toss shredded vegetable with two forks and fry for a few minutes until lightly cooked. Season with salt, pepper and nutmeg. Serve immediately.

Whilst this vegetable can be eaten raw, it tastes better if it is first blanched and it will also stay crisp longer. To do this, trim at top and bottom, plunge into boiling water for about 5 minutes, remove, drain and refresh in cold water. Dry and then slice or dice – at this point it may be marinated or simply dressed. The bland flavour of courgettes goes with many other vegetables, such as mushrooms, tomatoes, green peppers, olives and aubergines.

French Beans Boil whole if small or dice. Do not over-cook or colour and flavour will be spoiled.

Leeks Boil, braise or stir-fry very finely cut slices.

Lettuce Not often considered outside its role as a salad vegetable but there are times of the year when every salad grower has a surplus. They make a deliciously different vegetable washed, shredded and lightly tossed in butter and seasoned with sea salt and black pepper. Allow one lettuce per person. Other finely chopped or shredded vegetables (onion, carrot, parsley and so on) can be combined with the lettuce and stir-fried together.

Marrow Small cubes of young marrow are delicious, seasoned and stir-fried in butter until tender.

Mushrooms To bake: arrange the caps on a greased dish, dot each cap with butter, season, and bake in a moderate oven for 30–40 minutes. To fry: dip button mushrooms in seasoned butter and deep fry until crisp.

Onions Boil small onions and serve them in a light sauce; bake onions in honey, or deep fry onion rings. Finely sliced onions and finely shredded white cabbage can be stir-fried together gently in butter.

Parsnips Parboil, dip in flour, and deep fry as parsnip 'chips'. Boil and purée with cream, salt and black pepper.

Peas All sorts are delightful with trout, including mange-tout and sugar peas, very lightly cooked and still retaining some crispness in the pod.

Peppers Both tinned red peppers and sliced fresh red peppers can be used in the classic ratatouille, while whole peppers can be stuffed.

Potatoes Every way imaginable – this would take up a whole chapter!

Runner Beans Ideal boiled in salty water, but take care not to over-cook.

Sorrel Wash 900g/2lb freshly picked sorrel, cook rapidly in a little salted water for 5 minutes. Drain and chop as for spinach.

Spinach Cook as for sorrel. Serve coarsely chopped, puréed or for creamed spinach stir in a little thick cream just before serving.

Tomatoes Tomatoes can be presented baked, fried or stuffed. Tinned Italian tomatoes are useful, and you can thicken the juices with cornflour and season with salt, pepper, vinegar and a little brown sugar to make a sauce.

Turnips Little white turnips can be boiled until tender and served in a light sauce, or with a knob of butter.

Zucchini *See* Courgette.

APPENDIX

'Muddy' Flavour or Poor Condition?

Occasionally you will catch or acquire fish that do not look in the peak of condition. The silver belly of newly-stocked trout, for example, tends to turn greyish until the fish have been in their new surroundings for at least a week, and this is perhaps due to the shock of being transported. Sometimes, during a long spell of hot weather, water temperatures become uncomfortably high, and the fish do not taste their best. Even if this is the case, the fish are still perfectly edible, as long as the flesh and innards appear healthy, but they will need to be treated in one of the following ways:

Soak fish in strong salty water for 2 hours, then smoke cook. Use in pâté or soufflé recipe or serve in a curry sauce.

Clean, wash and dry the fish and fillet out bones. Mix a paste of 1 crushed garlic clove, ½ teaspoon turmeric, juice of ½ a lemon, salt and paprika, and 1 teaspoon olive oil or good vegetable oil. Coat all surfaces and leave to marinate for 2 hours. Fry or grill.

Soak in strong salty water for 2 hours, then pat dry and coat fish in strong savoury crumbs, either bought, or home-made as follows. Either grate stale bread, or keep all left-over toast and crusts and leave in the bottom of your oven to become baked as rusks in the general course of cooking other dishes. To these crumbs add either dried mixed herbs or crushed french onion soup mix. Finally, fry the fish in hot fat and serve with a large slice of lemon.

Fillet and soak fish in brine for 2 hours, and hang for approximately 24 hours in a cool, dust- and insect-free place. Cold smoke for 3–4 hours, and allow to mature for 24 hours before eating cold, or grilled with butter for a few minutes.

Clean and gut fish. Soak in brine for 2 hours, and then dry thoroughly with kitchen paper. Dust with flour and fry fish in light vegetable oil. Finally, pour a good tot of whisky into the pan, and serve piping hot.

Poach fish in ½ vinegar/½ water solution with plenty of salt. Allow to cool in liquor. Use in sandwiches or as part of an hors d'oeuvre, accompanied by horseradish or tartare sauce.

INDEX

Also from the Crowood Press:

THE GAME COOKBOOK

Carolyn Little

As game becomes more and more popular and widely available, Carolyn Little offers the reader over 150 delicious recipes, for both the beginner and those with some experience. This valuable addition to any kitchen bookshelf covers every aspect of cooking with game, including preparation and dressing, showing how versatile this meat can be. With line drawings and colour plates, The Game Cookbook opens the door to an original and challenging cuisine for every cook.

ISBN 1 85223 004 5

THE PHEASANT COOK

Tina Dennis and Rosamond Cardigan

This unique collection of 97 original and innovative recipes using the tastiest of game birds will be welcome in every cook's kitchen. The authors provide new inspiration, from soups and snacks to elaborate dinners, to help the reader tempt their family and their guests. Practical instruction and tips on hanging, plucking, drawing and trussing are included alongside a wealth of suggestions for mouthwatering dishes that make the best of every brace of pheasants.

ISBN 1 85223 198 X